# Trees and
# Shrubs

Chatto Nature Guides

# Trees and Shrubs

Illustrated and identified with colour
photographs

**Kurt Harz**

Translated and edited by
Gwynne Vevers

Chatto & Windus · London

Published by
Chatto & Windus Ltd.
40 William IV Street
London WC2N 4DF

*

Clarke, Irwin & Co Ltd.
Toronto

90143

ISBN 0 7011 2541 1   (Hardback)
ISBN 0 7011 2542 X   (Paperback)

Title of the original German edition:
*Bäume and Sträucher*

© BLV Verlagsgesellschaft mbH, München, 1979
English Translation © Chatto & Windus Ltd 1980

Printed in Germany

# Introduction

Trees and shrubs are important in several different ways. Their aesthetic importance can be easily assessed if one merely imagines a well-known landscape without them: all that is left is a barren expanse of steppe. In former times this happened when certain areas of southern Europe and northern Africa were completely deforested. Weather and the activities of sheep and goats saw to it that the trees did not return. These barren areas of the Mediterranean are a sharp reminder of the immense importance that trees and shrubs have in shaping our environment. They purify the air, reduce the force of the wind and delay the seepage of water, for trees soak it up like a sponge, later releasing it to the environment.

A medium-sized deciduous tree has approximately 200,000 leaves, with an enormous surface area. For instance, a Beech tree with about 150,000 leaves, each with an average surface area of 20 square centimetres, has a surface for evaporation of 300 square metres. Thus, in a single summer's day, one hectare of Beech woodland will produce 30,000 litres of water by evaporation. With such enormous surface woodland trees not only release water, but also free oxygen produced during the process of photosynthesis, so it is most appropriate that parks and woodland in and around large human settlements have been referred to as "green lungs". Furthermore, woods and hedges provide a suitable habitat and food for a vast number of living organisms, and they yield many wild fruits, berries and fungi for human consumption.

A natural wood or forest forms a biological community in which each constituent part is dependent upon the others. The biological equilibrium is easily disrupted, and unfortunately this has often happened as a result of human interference. Afforestation programmes in certain areas have altered the composition of woodlands and in some cases this has been allowed to get the upper hand.

In addition to the recreational value of trees and shrubs, particularly in large cities, there is also the economic aspect. Trees are still widely used for building, furniture, textiles, paper, resin, gas, tanning agents and medicinal drugs.

The woodlands of Europe were not always like those we know today. At one time familiar trees such as Maple or shrubs like Elder were growing alongside Magnolias, Trumpet Flowers, which nowadays we only know as introduced and much valued garden plants. Before about 30,000 years ago, vast areas of Europe had only a covering of low-growing vegetation, such as Dwarf Birch (*Betula nana*) mostly about 50cm in height, and still to be found in upland areas of Europe and North America; it is also a typical sub-shrub in the ice-free areas of Greenland. Later on, from about 20,000 B.C. to 12,000 B.C. the dominant trees in Europe were various pines and birches, and from 12,000 B.C. to 4,000 B.C., Hazel, as the climate became warmer. From then until about 1,800 B.C. the vegetation was dominated by Oak, Lime, Maple and Elm. Finally, the Late Stone Age saw the rise of Beech, which colonized wide areas that are subject to an Atlantic climate; this handsome tree was probably at its peak about 800 B.C.

Among modern trees and shrubs there are still some dwarfs, such as the Wild Azalea (*Loiseleuria procumbens*), a low-growing sub-shrub about 10-30cm long which has a circumpolar distribution and is also found as a relict in the Alps and the Scottish Highlands. Some specimens of this plant with a stem diameter of 10mm are 70 years or more old. The tallest trees are the giant *Eucalyptus* of Australia which reach a height of 155m. The oldest tree in Europe is probably a Yew growing in Kent which has been established as 2,500 years old. In North America there is a colony, only 2km across, of *Gaylussacia*, a relative of the whortleberries. These plants are estimated to be 13,000 years old.

There are plenty of other fascinating aspects of trees and shrubs, but this book is primarily intended to assist in identification. It covers the principal species of trees to be found in Britain, giving their main characteristics, in particular those which help to distinguish one species from another. Some of these trees are native, others have been introduced, mostly during the last 500 years. The book also includes a number of smaller shrubs which grow wild in Europe, but it does not attempt to cover the very numerous ornamental shrubs which play an ever-increasing part in parks and gardens.

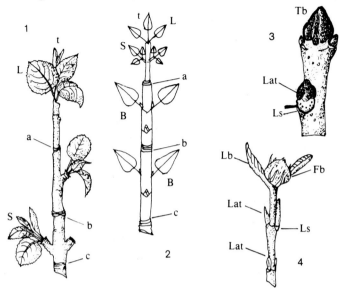

## The anatomy of trees and shrubs

A tree consists of a trunk and crown, whereas a shrub has no main trunk, but several stems growing up from near ground level. The roots often extend over an area corresponding to that covered by the aerial parts of the tree of shrubs.

The trunk or stems produce branches which themselves give rise to long or short shoots. Long shoots usually grow from a terminal bud and are responsible for growth in length (fig. 1 shows a long shoot, fig. 2 the same in diagrammatic form). Lateral buds are mainly concerned with the production of short shoots. These produce the leaves and often also the flowers, as in Apple and Pear. Sometimes, as in Barberry, the short shoots are very short. Because leaves and shoots arise from buds their positions always correspond (see the figures in the key on pp. 17-24). This arrangement is constant within genera, or even within a whole plant family, so that the crown of a free-standing tree may have such a characteristic appearance that one can identify the species at a distance; this would not necessarily be true if the tree were growing in close-packed, crowded conditions in a forest. The age of a shoot or its annual growth can usually be easily determined, because the shed scales of the terminal bud always leave a ring or band of typical scars. In figs. 1 and 2, t = this year's shoot which will become woody in the course of the year, a = the start of the previous year's growth, b = the start of the 2-year old growth, c = the start of the 3-year old growth, while L = leaf, S = short shoot, and B = bud.

The shape of the leaf is of immense importance as an aid to the identification of trees and shrubs. A leaf is said to be entire when its margin shows no indentations, dentate or toothed when the margin has short or shallow indentations, and lobed when the margin is more deeply indented.or divided, but without the incisions reaching the midrib or the leaf stalk (*petiole*). A simple leaf has only a single blade. A compound leaf is one in which the leaf blade is divided to the midrib or petiole, producing separate leaflets. When there are more than three leaflets the leaf is feathered or pinnate (e.g. Common Ash, p. 130). When the leaflets diverge from a common point the leaf is said to be fingered or digitate (e.g. Horse Chestnut, p. 110). The margin of a leaf is ciliate when it is bordered with hairs or fine hair-like teeth. These and other terms are illustrated in the key to the genera.

Less attention has been paid to the flowers and fruits of trees and shrubs, because these have been frequently illustrated and in this book emphasis has been laid on the leaves and their arrangement as aids to identification.

As already mentioned, the position of the buds on a shoot corresponds exactly with that of the leaves. The buds are usually enclosed in leafy scales the numbers of which vary considerably. There are also naked buds, i.e. those without scales as in the Wayfaring Tree (fig. 4). The abbreviations in figs. 3 and 4 are: Fb = flower bud, Lat = lateral bud, Lb = leaf bud, Ls = leaf scar, Tb = terminal bud. Leaf scars are left when the leaf stalk or petioles become detached as the leaves fall, usually in late autumn; they may be very characteristic diagnostic characters (see the key to buds on pp. 17-24).

## Notes on the text from p. 26

Frequent use is made of the term "at first". This refers to the appearance of a structure, such as bark, in the early part of the year, and not in late summer or early autumn.

8

# Key to the genera

Start with the first pair of alternatives and select the one that applies to the tree or shrub that you are trying to identify. Your choice leads to a number, in this case either 5 or 2, on the right hand side of the page. Find this number on the left hand side of the page, and from the pair of alternatives that follows it select the one that applies to your specimen; and repeat the process until it leads you to the name of a tree or shrub.

The figures in brackets refer to the drawings on pp. 9-16.

**1** Leaves not needle-shaped, nor very short and narrow **-5**
— Leaves needle-shaped **-2**
    (in the case of very small shrubs, 15-45cm tall, with
    needle-shaped or very narrow leaves 2-5mm long, see
    Ling, p. 128, and Cross-leaved Heath, p. 128)
**2** Needles not continuing down the stem as ridges **-3**
— Needles decurrent (continuing down stem as green
    ridges) (5) **Yew, p. 26**
**3** Needles not in clusters on short shoots **-4**
— Needles in clusters on short shoots **Larch, p. 32**
**4** Needles in bunches of 2, 3 or 5 with a short basal sheath
    (6) **Scots Pine, p. 36**
    or in whorls of 3 **Juniper, p. 38**
— Needles single, 4-sided, pointed with brown stalks (7)
    **Norway Spruce, p. 30**
    or flat, with green stalks (8) **Silver Fir, p. 28**

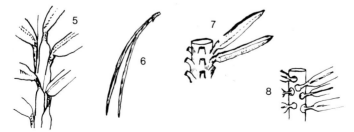

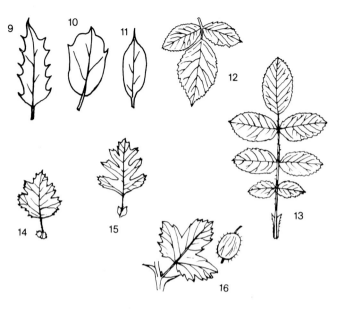

**5** Not thorny, not twining nor climbing      **-19**
— Thorny, twining or climbing      **-6**
**6** Climbing or twining      **-16**
— With thorns or prickles      **-7**
**7** Leaf tough, leathery, sharply toothed or with sharp tip
     (9-11)      **Holly, p. 102**
— Leaf not so      **-8**
**8** Leaf 3-lobed (12) or pinnate (13)      **-14**
     (or if a shrub only 30-50cm tall, the stem with 1-2
     rows of hairs, the leaflets ovate to longish, toothed,
     see Restharrow, p. 98)
— Leaf simple, i.e. with only 1 blade      **-9**
**9** Leaf not lobed      **-10**
— Leaf with 3-5 lobes (14, 15)      **Hawthorn, p. 82**
     (if thorns in groups of usually 3 (16), see Gooseberry,
     p. 72)

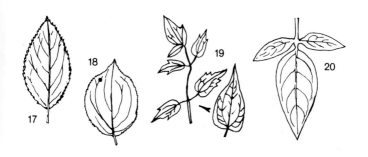

**10** Three-lobed thorns below the short shoots

**Barberry, p. 72**

— Thorns otherwise **-11**

**11** Leaf finely toothed **-12**

— Leaf entire, the underside with silvery scales

**Sea Buckthorn, p. 118**

**12** Leaf upperside not shiny dark green **-13**

— Leaf upperside shiny dark green **Pear, p. 74**

**13** Basal veins not reaching distal third of leaf (17)

**Blackthorn, p. 94**

(or if leaf usually over 5cm long and thorns weak, see Plum, p. 94)

— Basal veins reaching distal third of leaf (18)

**Common Blackthorn, p. 112**

**14** Leaf with 3-11 toothed leaflets, thorns single **-15**

— Leaf with 7-19 entire leaflets, thorns in pairs at base of bud or petiole **Locust Tree, p. 96**

**15** Leaflets 3-8, petiole base with filamentous to lanceolate stipules **Rubus spp., p. 84**

— Leaflets usually 5-11, petiole base with broad stipules

**Dog Rose, p. 88**

**16** Leaf simple **-18**

— Leaf compound **-17**

**17** Leaves all with 3-9 long-stalked leaflets, terminal leaflet not strikingly larger (19) **Traveller's Joy, p. 70**

— Only upper leaves with 3 leaflets, the terminal one much larger than lateral leaflets (20) **Bittersweet, p. 132**

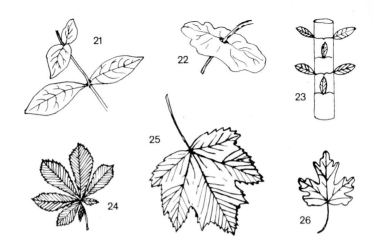

**18** Leaves opposite or the upper ones fused in pairs, entire
(21, 22)                    **Perfoliate Honeysuckle, p. 138**
— Leaves alternate, those on non-flowering or non-fruiting
shoots heart-shaped at base with 3-5 angles
**Ivy, p. 120**
**19** Leaves and buds not opposite                    **-32**
— Leaves and buds opposite (23)                    **-20**
**20** Small shrubs not growing on trees                    **-21**
— Small shrubs growing on trees          **Mistletoe, p. 68**
**21** Leaves longer than 2cm                    **-22**
— Small shrubs with leaves 2-8mm long (or leaves strongly
scented when rubbed, roundish-elliptical, 5-15mm, see
Thyme, p. 98)                    **Heaths, p. 128**
**22** Leaf simple                    **-25**
— Leaf compound                    **-23**
**23** Leaf pinnate                    **-24**
— Leaf digitae with (3-) 4-9 leaflets (24)
**Horse Chestnut, p. 110**
**24** Branches without soft, white to yellow-brown bark, a
tree                    **Ash, p. 130**
— Branches with soft, white to yellow-brown bark, usually
a shrub                    **Elder, p. 134**
**25** Leaf not lobed                    **-27**
— Leaf lobed                    **-26**

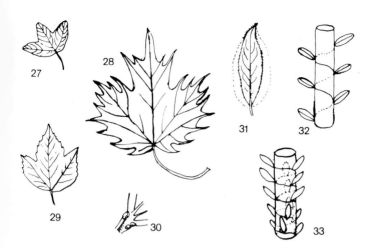

**26** Petiole upperside not furrowed, leaf as figs. 25-28
**Maples, p. 106**
— Petiole upperside deeply furrowed, with glands (30), leaf
as fig. 29       **Guelder Rose, p. 136**
**27** Leaf underside without grey to white down   **-28**
— Leaf underside with grey to white down
**Wayfaring Tree, p. 136**
**28** Leaf underside without yellow glands, the margin not
ciliate       **-29**
— Leaf underside with yellow glands, the margin ciliate
**Rhododendron, p. 124**
**29** Leaf entire       **-30**
— Leaf finely toothed (31)       **Spindle-tree, p. 104**
**30** Leaf underside not downy, shoots smooth   **-31**
— Leaf underside and shoots downy
**Fly Honeysuckle, p. 138**
**31** Leaf elliptical-ovate       **Dogwood, p. 122**
— Leaf longish-lanceolate       **Privet, p. 132**
**32** Leaves and buds arranged in two rows (32)   **-33**
— Leaves and buds arranged spirally or apparently
irregularly (33)       **-37**
**33** Leaf distinctly toothed       **-35**
— Leaf entire or at the most indistinctly toothed   **-34**

**34** Leaf underside with rust-coloured scales
**Rhododendron, p. 124**
— Leaf underside without scales       **Beech, p. 60**
**35** Leaf slightly asymmetrical, may be heart-shaped (34) **-36**
— Leaf very asymmetrical (35), seed a broadly winged nut
    (36-38)                     **Elms, p. 66**
**36** Leaf not heart-shaped (39)
**Hazel, p. 52, Hornbeam, p. 50**
— Leaf heart-shaped (34)          **Limes, p. 114**
**37** Large trees or shrubs, if small then the leaves are over
    3cm long or unlike those of the following    **-40**
— Small shrubs (10-50cm tall) with leaves up to 2.5cm
    long, if a larger shrub then with evergreen leaves, or
    if leaves are longer then petiole with hairy fringe  **-38**
**38** Petiole not hairy                      **-39**
— Petiole with hairy fringe (40)   **Mountain Avens, p. 86**
**39** Leaf tip without a spine    **Bilberries, etc., p. 126**
    (if leaflets are lanceolate, see Dyer's Greenweed, p.
    98)
— Leaf tip with a tiny spine (41, 42)
**Shrubby Milkwort, p. 100**
    (if a larger shrub, see Box, p. 100)
**40** Leaf simple                          **-41**
— Leaf compound                     **-54**
**41** Leaf not entire                      **-43**
— Leaf entire                         **-42**
**42** Leaf broadly-elliptical, usually pointed (43)
**Alder Buckthorn, p. 112**
— Leaf Lanceolate, narrowing towards the base (44)
**Mezereon, p. 118**
**43** Leaf not lobed, only toothed            **-46**
— Leaf lobed                       **-44**
**44** Leaf underside with white down, lobes toothed  **-45**
— Leaf underside with white down, lobes not toothed
**White Poplar, p. 40**
**45** Leaf usually much longer than broad (45-48)
**Oaks, p. 62**
    (if lobes are toothed, see Swedish Whitebeam, p. 78)
— Leaf scarcely longer than broad (49)
**Wild Service Tree, p. 78**
**46** Leaf underside not downy to hairy       **-48**
— Leaf underside downy to hairy          **-47**

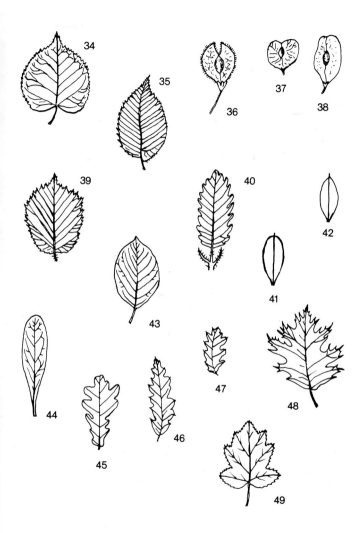

34

35

36

37

38

39

40

41

42

43

44

45

46

47

48

49

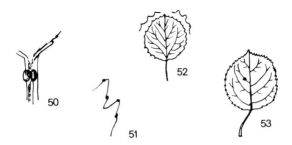

**47** Leaf underside with white down     **Whitebeams, p. 78**
    (if leaf is 6-12cm long, longish-lanceolate to longish-
    ovate, finely toothed, see Medlar, p. 82)
— Leaf ovate-elliptical to linear, often pointed, the
    underside whitish to bluish-green     **Willows, p. 46**
**48** Petiole often with glands (50), leaf teeth with glands (51)
                               **Cherries, p. 90**
— Petiole without glands, leaf teeth without glands     **-49**
**49** Leaf roundish, diamond-shaped or triangular, not
    toothed, without a narrow, translucent margin     **-50**
— Leaf roundish, diamond-shaped or triangular, toothed
    (52) or with a narrow, translucent margin
                               **Poplars, p. 40**
**50** Leaf upperside not shiny green     **-51**
— Leaf upperside shiny green, ovate to roundish, petiole
    half as long or as long as the leaf     **Pear, p. 74**
    (if leaf is narrow, several times as long as broad with
    a short petiole, see Willows, p. 46)
**51** Trees without white bark     **-52**
— Trees with white bark     **Birch, p. 54**
**52** Leaf pointed-ovate, with more than 4 pairs of veins     **-53**
— Leaf usually with only 4 pairs of veins (53)   **Apple, p. 76**
**53** Leaf simple, irregularly toothed, sometimes sticky, the
    underside never with white down     **Alder, p. 58**
— Leaf toothed, a small tree or shrub with ovate leaves,
    the underside with white down at first
                           **Snowy Mespilus, p. 86**
    (if a larger tree with ovate, pointed to longish-ovate
    leaves, see Plums, p. 94)
**54** Leaflets entire, aromatic when rubbed     **Walnut, p. 64**
— Leaflets toothed, not aromatic
                 **Rowan or True Service Tree, p. 80**

# Buds as an aid to identification

In Britain and in Europe north of the Alps buds are regarded as a symbol of spring, but are otherwise more or less neglected. This is unfortunate because not only do they provide an aid to identification, but also they are interesting and attractive. Many of the buds shown in the drawings on pp. 17-24 are also mentioned in the main text starting on p. 26.

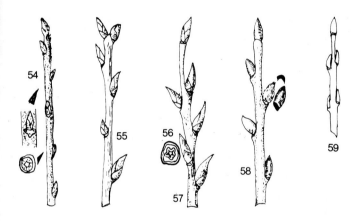

**54** White Poplar. Left, a single bud, and below it a
    transverse section of a twig.
**55** Aspen. Leaf buds long, wedge-shaped. Flower buds (on
    older trees) ovate
**56** Black Poplar. Transverse section of a twig to show 5-
    cornered core
**57** Black Poplar
**58** Sallow; the single scale can be detached like a cap
**59** Purple Willow, with opposite buds

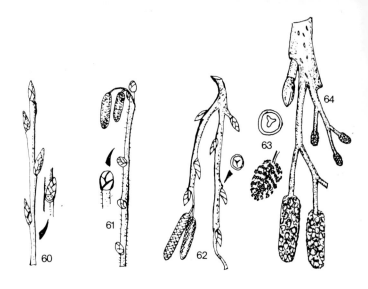

**60** Hornbeam

**61** Hazel; before flowering the male catkins are much longer

**62** Downy Birch; right, transverse section through a twig to show 3-cornered core

**63** Common Alder; transverse section through a twig to show 3-cornered core

**64** Common Alder, with male and female catkins; left a fruit from which the seeds have already fallen.

**65** Green Alder, with male and female catkins and transverse section of twig.

**66** Grey Alder

**67** Common Beech; beneath the 3 buds is the scar left by the previous year's terminal bud

**68** Sessile Oak, transverse section of a twig

**69** Sessile Oak

**70** Walnut; at the bottom the twig has been sliced open to show the core.

**71** Smooth-leafed Elm with leaf and flower buds

**72** Wych Elm; right, a bud enlarged

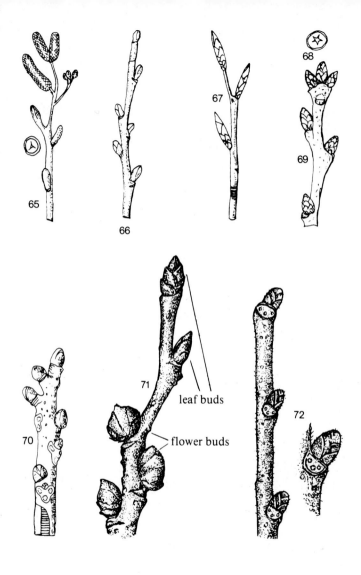

65

66

67

68

69

70

71

leaf buds

flower buds

72

19

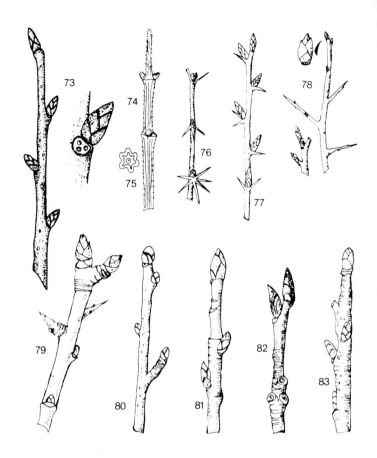

**73** European White Elm; right, a bud enlarged
**74** Traveller's Joy
**75** Traveller's Joy, transverse section through a shoot
**76** Barberry, showing spines
**77** Gooseberry
**78** Common Pear, top left a terminal bud
**79** Crab Apple
**80** Wild Service Tree
**81** Whitebeam
**82** Rowan
**83** True Service Tree

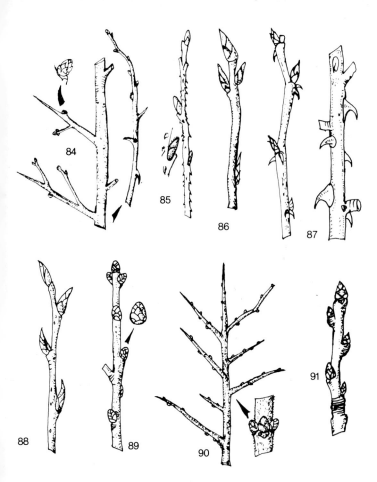

**84** Midland Hawthorn
**85** Bramble
**86** Snowy Mespilus
**87** Dog Rose: different development of spines on young
and old twigs
**88** Bird Cherry
**89** Wild Cherry
**90** Blackthorn; right, three buds above a leaf scar
**91** Plum

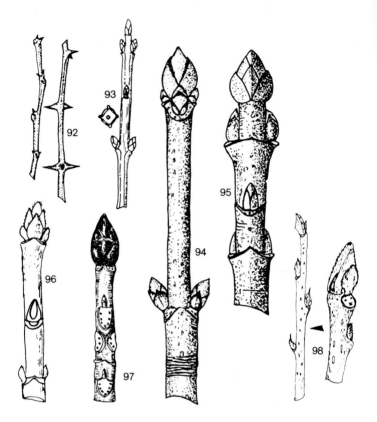

**92** Locust Tree; left, a twig from a tree, right, from a shrub. Thorns on younger shoots are even longer.

**93** Spindle-tree; left, transverse section through a twig to show the 4 corky ridges.

**94** Sycamore; below, last year's scar ring

**95** Norway Maple

**96** Field Maple

**97** Horse Chestnut, but its natural size would be 3-4 times larger

**98** Alder Buckthorn; left, in spring with the lateral buds already sprouting; right, in deep winter with the lateral buds still considerably smaller than the terminal bud

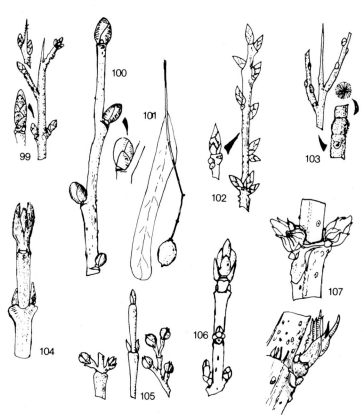

99 Buckthorn
100 Small-leafed Lime; right, the same bud as on the twig, but seen from the other side.
101 Small-leafed Lime, showing a single fruit (the other has already fallen) and the bract
102 Mezereon
103 Sea Buckthorn; right, a bud enlarged and a scale much enlarged
104 Dogwood
105 Cornelian Cherry
106 Privet
107 Elder; above, in winter; below, in early spring with leaf sprouts already showing

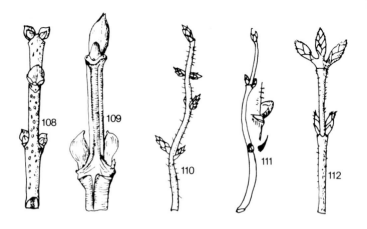

**108** Red-berried Elder
**109** Guelder Rose
**110** Perfoliate Honeysuckle
**111** Honeysuckle
**112** Fly Honeysuckle

# Trees and
# Shrubs

# Yew *Taxus baccata*

**Characteristics:** an evergreen shrub or tree, growing to a height of 25 m, with a roundish to ovate crown; the shape may be irregular, particularly if the trunk is much branched. The bark is reddish-brown to purplish, shedding scaly fragments as the tree grows. On the erect shoots the leaves are arranged spirally, on side shoots usually in a row along each side. Each leaf is linear, ending in a sharp point, and 2-4 cm long, 2-3 mm wide; the base is short (fig. 5). Leaves are deep dark green above with a distinct midrib, those on young shoots more yellow-green. The trees are either male or female. Flowering takes place in February-April. The male flowers are small and spherical and they appear singly on the underside of the previous year's shoots. Female flowers are very small and green and at first difficult to discern. Each produces a single seed surrounded by a conspicuous fleshy red aril (opposite). A very slow-growing tree.—**Distribution:** tolerates shade and so often grows in the undergrowth below deciduous and coniferous trees. A lime-loving tree distributed throughout Europe, at altitudes up to 1,800 m. A large number of varieties exist and these can be seen in parks and gardens.

Yew contains the poison taxin which brings about cardiac arrest. It is said that 500 g of the leaves will kill a horse. Ruminants, however, tolerate much more and Roe Deer even have a liking for Yew shoots. The sweetish, slimy aril is not poisonous, but the hard seed is.

Yews grow to a great age and some are certainly 1,000 years old, occasionally much more. In the past they were frequently planted in churchyards and were once much valued for making bows.

# Common Silver Fir  *Abies alba*

**Characteristics:** an evergreen tree growing to a height of c. 50 m and therefore with the Norway Spruce (below, left) the largest native conifer in Europe. The crown is symmetrical. In old trees the bole at a height of 1.5 m has a diameter of 2 m. The bark is smooth and greyish. The branches grow out horizontally from the trunk. Growth in height ceases after c. 100 years and the side branches then grow upwards. The leaves or needles, which are up to 2 cm long, are arranged in two rows with several layers on each side of the shoot (opposite, above). They are shiny dark green above with a longitudinal furrow, and with two whitish longitudinal bands below. The leaf stalk is very short and enlarged to form a disc (fig. 8). The leaves fall off after 7-11 years, leaving smooth shoots. The buds are ovate, red-brown, non-resinous or slightly resinous. Flowering takes place in May-June. The male flowers are small and spherical, arranged densely along the underside of the previous year's shoots. The cones, which are c. 10-15 cm long and 4 cm across, grow erect on the upperside of branches close to the crown of the tree. They are green in summer, becoming orange-brown in September, and have large scales and also bracts which turns downwards. The scales fall off after the release of the seeds.—**Distribution:** Europe, including France, Corsica, Germany, the Alps, Tatra and the Balkan Mountains. Not native to Britain, but formerly much planted. Old trees are not uncommon in Scotland, north-western England, Devon and Cornwall. Nowadays the very similar Grand Fir (*Abies grandis*), Noble Fir (*A. procera*) and Caucasian Fir (*A. nordmanniana*) are more commonly grown in forestry plantations in Britain.

In Scotland Common Silver Firs have a life span of 300 years, in England rarely 200 years.

# Norway Spruce  *Picea abies*

**Characteristics:** an evergreen tree, 30-50 m in height with a bole diameter of 2 m. The crown is conical (p. 29, below, left) with the branches arranged in whorls growing out horizontally or upwards in the upper half of the tree, but more downwards in the lower half. When growing in uncrowded conditions the whole trunk is well furnished with branches, but in dense plantations the lower branches die off. The trunk is straight and columnar, the bark is reddish-brown, in the mountains more greyish, shredding into fine scales. The roots are quite shallow. The leaves or needles are 1-3 cm long and 4 mm broad, four-sided and ending in a hard point. The leaves grow out each side of the shoot and above it. When the needles fall off they leave the brown basal part so that the twig is rough to the touch (fig. 7). The buds are slender and brown, not resinous. Flowering takes place in May. The spherical male flowers are at first crimson and then yellow and they shed copious amounts of sulphur-yellow pollen; they appear at the tips of the previous year's shoots on old trees. In young trees the female flowers appear on the upper whorls, but in older trees they may be seen all over the crown. The cones are at first red and erect, but they soon hang down and become green. They ripen after a year and are then brown (p. 29, below, right), 10-15 cm long and 3-4 cm across.—**Distribution:** Europe from Scandinavia to the Alps, the Balkans and Russia. Introduced to Britain, probably about 500 years ago, and now familiar as Christmas trees. A commonly planted tree in large gardens and forestry plantations, particularly in areas with a heavy rainfall. There are several cultivated varieties.

Norway Spruce have a rapid rate of growth when young, and they have a life span of about 200 years.

# European Larch  *Larix decidua*

**Characteristics:** a deciduous coniferous tree with a straight, slender trunk and a narrow, conical crown, growing to a height of c. 40 m (above, left) with the main branches horizontal and arranged in whorls. The bark is greenish grey-brown and at first smooth, but soon becomes slightly furrowed and more greyish, finally being pinkish-brown and scaly. The shoots are yellow or pinkish. The needles are soft, green and flat above, keeled and grey-green below, up to 4 cm long. On new shoots they grow singly, on short spurs of last year's growth in bunches of 23-40 (above, right), being pale green at first, becoming darker in summer, and golden in the autumn when they fall off. The buds are pale brown. Flowering occurs in April-June, usually at intervals of 3-5 years. The male flowers are ovate to spherical and appear on the underside of the shoots as whitish discs which later become yellow when the pollen is being shed. The female flowers are at the end of shoots, surrounded by leaves, and are purplish (below, left); they open about 14 days before the male flowers. The cones are at first green, but ripen to brown in the same year. They are ovate, somewhat rounded, 2-4 cm long and 2-3 cm across, with rounded scales (below, right). In some the dead cones remain on the tree for about ten years.—**Distribution:** originally the Alps, Sudeten, Tatra Mountains, parts of Poland and the Carpathians, at altitudes of 1,000-3,000 m. Introduced into Britain in the early 17th century and now common in many parts, preferring deep lime or clay soils, but also growing in poorer soils, and requiring good light. There are several varieties. The closely related and very similar Japanese Larch (*Larix kaempferi*) came to Britain in the late 19th century and is now extensively planted in western, hilly districts.

# Mountain Pine *Pinus uncinata* and *P. mugo*

**Characteristics:** an evergreen tree up to 20 m in height (*P. uncinata*) but also occurring as a straggling shrub (*P. mugo*) (above). The bark is grey-brown to blackish grey-brown with red markings, and scaly, breaking into irregular plates. Young shoots are at first pale green, then dark brown. The needles are in pairs and dark green and curved, and 3-4 (-8) cm long and 1 mm across, and pointed. Buds are longish-ovate, pointed, about 5 mm long and very resinous. Flowering takes place in June-July, the male flowers being yellow, the female purple (below, left). The cones are shiny, almost terminal, up to four together, erect to slightly pendant, 2-6 cm long, 1.5-4.0 cm across; the seeds are only released after two years.—**Distribution:** a lime-loving, ice age relict from the Alps, Pyrenees, Carpathians, Balkans and Abruzzi. Often planted in gardens and also used to consolidate dunes.

# Austrian Pine *Pinus nigra*

**Characteristics:** an evergreen conifer 20-40 m in height (below, right) with a conical crown, which becomes more umbrella-shaped with age. The bark is dark brown or dark grey, with coarse ridges and scaly. The straight or curved needles, growing in pairs, are 8-14 cm long, 3 mm across, within sheaths which are 10-12 mm long. The buds are ovate to cylindrical, pointed, pale reddish-brown and resinous. The flowers appear in June-July, the males in groups of 3-10 on young shoots, the females singly or in groups at the tips of the same shoots. The cones which are up to 8 cm long, 4 cm across and shiny yellow-brown to pale brown, do not release the seeds until the third year.—**Distribution:** growing on poor, limey soils from the Mediterranean area and Austria to the Caspian Sea. Technically the Austrian Pine is *P. nigra* var. *nigra*, the Corsican Pine is *P. nigra* var. *maritima*. Both forms are commonly planted in gardens and parks in Britain, where they grow very well.

# Scots Pine  *Pinus sylvestris*

**Characteristics:** an evergreen conifer, 10-35 m in height. Depending upon the locality, soil and climate the trunk may be more or less straight (above, left) or stunted with a broader crown (above, right). The bark of the young trees is pale grey or orange-red, but is reddish-brown in older trees with deep furrows and thick plates. The bole circumference may be up to 5 m. The stiff needles grow in pairs in sheaths 8 mm long (fig. 6). The needles gradually become shorter as the tree ages; those on trees 2-3 years old are 4-7 cm long, 2 mm across, pointed, usually somewhat curved and bluish-green or grey-green. Buds are longish-ovate, 6-12 mm long and reddish-brown. Flowering takes place in May-June. Male flowers are yellow and at the base of weaker young shoots. Female flowers, 1-5 together, on stronger young shoots, are at first pink, then green, and finally brown and pendant. The cone scales facing the light are usually larger than those facing the tree. The cones are 2.5-7.0 cm long and 2.0-3.5 cm across (below, left and right) and may remain on the tree for 2-3 years.—**Distribution:** throughout Europe and eastwards to the Amur region, even growing on sand or in rocky places. In the Alps extending up to altitudes of 1,800 m, sometimes more. There are geographical varieties and also numerous cultivated forms. The life span is about 250-300 years.

The Arolla Pine (*P. cembra*) is an evergreen tree 10-20 m in height. The crown is conical or columnar and there are often horizontal branches almost down to ground level. The bark is grey-green with red-brown fissures, becoming grey-brown with age. In their first year the shoots are yellowish. The stiff needles, in groups of five, are 5-12 cm long, 1 mm across, with a very finely toothed edge. Young cones are purple, but are red-brown when ripe. The seeds are 12 mm long, 6-7 mm across and edible (pine nuts). Originally Alps and Carpathians, but planted in parks and gardens.

# Common Juniper  *Juniperus communis*

**Characteristics:** an evergreen small tree, up to 15 m in height, usually with several stems, but more common as a 3-5 m tall shrub, very variable in shape. The bark is at first grey-brown and smooth, later becoming scaly. The young shoots are triangular in cross section, with longitudinal ridges. The leaves or needles grow in whorls of three. They are c. 10 mm long, 1-2 mm across, sharply pointed, grey-green on the upperside. Flowering takes place in June-July. The male flowers, which grow on separate trees from the females, are ovate, terminal, on short shoots or axillary. Female flowers are spherical with a short scaly stem. The fruits are green in the first year, then bluish and finally in the second or third they are blackish spheres (below, right) with dry, very aromatic flesh and each contains three seeds.—**Distribution:** Europe, North America, North Africa and parts of Asia. A native plant in Britain where it grows mostly on chalk or limestone, but in Scotland it can be found growing in shallow peat. There is a dwarf form which grows in mountains up to altitudes of 1,600-3,000 m; it scarcely reaches a height of 20-30 cm.

Several other species are cultivated in Europe. One of the commonest of these is the Chinese Juniper (*J. chinensis*) which grows well in parks, gardens and churchyards.

Juniper berries are, of course, used in cookery and also to flavour gin.

# Poplars  *Populus*

Deciduous, fast-growing trees, nearly all with male and female flowers on different trees. The flowers appear before the foliage and they are pollinated by wind. The fruit capsules release numerous fluffy seeds.

## White Poplar  *Populus alba*

**Characteristics:** a tree growing to c. 30 m in height in 30-40 years, with a diameter of 1 m. The life span is 300-400 years and the trunk would then have a diameter of 2-4 m. The crown is usually broadly rounded and leaning to one side. The bark is at first pale to dark grey-green, the youngest shoots whitish. With age the bark becomes blackish-grey to black. The shoots are green covered with white wool when new, pale brown in the second year. The leaves on strong growth have 3-5 lobes, measure $12 \times 20$ cm, and are coated beneath with white down. On shorter shoots and on the underside of the strong shoots the leaves are ovate to roundish, irregularly toothed, more greyish beneath, c. $4\text{-}7 \times 3\text{-}4$ cm. The leaf stalk or petiole is flat, 3-4 cm long and hairy. The buds are orange-brown with small white hairs (fig. 54). Flowering is in March-April, the catkins being 4-8 cm, the males reddish to yellow, the females pale green.—**Distribution:** central and southern Europe eastwards to central Asia, preferring sites near rivers, but it also thrives in other deep soils in good light. Introduced in Britain, where it is quite common in parks, gardens and roadsides. It produces numerous suckers which help to bind soil in e.g. dune country. Female trees are rare.

The Grey Poplar (*P. canescens*) is a hybrid between the White Poplar and the Aspen (pp. 42-43). It is similar to the White Poplar but the young shoots are more greyish. The leaves are very variable in shape, the undersides at first with grey hairs, later slightly shiny and pale green. It has the same distribution as the White Poplar and is probably not native to Britain, but is locally common.

# Aspen *Populus tremula*

**Characteristics:** a tree 20-30 m in height, with a trunk diameter of c. 1 m. The crown is at first often conical, later roundish to irregular. The bark is greenish-rey to yellowish-grey and smooth, later with some ridges. The trees produce suckers which grow into dense bushes. The shoots are dark brown and shiny. The leaves are broadly ovate to roundish with irregular, blunt teeth (fig. 52) and they measure 3-7 × 3.0 cm. They are at first slightly hairy, brownish to reddish, soon becoming shiny and green. On the suckers the leaves are ovate, up to 15 cm long, the underside hairy. Petioles are thin, flat, as long as the leaves, which move with the slightest breath of wind, hence the expression "to tremble like an aspen leaf". The first leaves in spring do not tremble and they have nectar glands which attract ants. The leaf buds (fig. 55) are pale to dark brown, often greenish or grey at the base of the scales, the terminal bud being ovate-conical, 1-10 mm long. The catkin buds are ovate and pointed, shiny resinous and red-brown. Flowering takes place in March-April. The male catkins are at first grey-brown to silvery-brown becoming yellowish when the pollen is being shed. Female catkins are green.—**Distribution:** Europe and western Asia, on loam and sandy soils, in open woodland, and along the edges of woods where the light is good. A native tree in Britain, where it is particularly common in the north and west of Scotland, less so in south-eastern England. The life span may be about 100 years.

# Black Poplar *Populus nigra*

**Characteristics:** a tree up to 30 m in height with a broad, spreading crown (above, left). The trunk has a diameter of up to 2 m. One-year shoots are yellowish to yellow-grey, becoming grey in the second year; in cross section they show a 5-cornered core (fig. 56). The bark is greyish with short ridges. The leaf is roughly triangular, with a long point and rounded sides (above, right), finely toothed, the edges translucent, and measuring 5-10 × 3-8 cm. The autumn colour is yellow. The petiole is flattened, shiny and somewhat shorter than the leaf. Buds (fig. 57) are ovate-conical, usually with three scales, sticky and scented, and chestnut-brown. Flowering takes place in March-April, the male catkins at first grey, becoming reddish, the females greenish-white. The white woolly seeds are shed in June.—**Distribution:** Europe and western Asia, with several varieties. One variety is native to Britain. This tree prefers loose sandy and clay soils and it often grows close to rivers. It has been much planted to shield factories and playing-fields. There are numerous hybrid Black Poplars (hybrids between *P. nigra* and two American species).

The most remarkable form of *P. nigra* is the Lombardy Poplar (below) with its tall, columnar growth, which is due to the upright growth of the branches. It came originally from northern Italy and was introduced into Britain in 1758. It is propagated by cuttings from male trees, as female trees are very rare.

# Willows  *Salix*

Trees or shrubs, sometimes tiny and creeping. The leaves are narrow, up to 15 times as long as they are wide, or ovate, elliptical to roundish, and almost always arranged spirally. The buds are enclosed in a single scale which can be removed like a cap (fig. 58). The male and female flowers are on separate trees. Flowering takes place in March-April, usually with erect catkins and pollination is by insects, including bees. Some nineteen species are native to Britain, with numerous hybrids and varieties.

# White Willow  *Salix alba*

**Characteristics:** a tree 6-25 m in height, with a trunk diameter of up to 1 m. The crown is much branched, with young shoots hanging over the tips of older branches often hanging right over (above, left). The bark is brownish-grey to dark grey with thick close-set ridges. The leaves are lanceolate, finely toothed, measuring 6-10 × 1-1.5 cm, the undersides always with dense silky down, giving the tree a silvery appearance when the leaves are moved by the wind.—**Distribution:** Europe, North Africa, eastwards to central Asia. Native in most parts of Britain. The numerous varieties of this tree include the Weeping Willow and the Cricket-bat Willow which is grown commercially in East Anglia.

# Sallow  *Salix caprea*

**Characteristics:** also known as Goat Willow or Pussy Willow, this is a tree about 10 m in height (above, right), but often only a tall shrub, with grey-green bark. The leaves are broadly elliptical, often with conspicuous yellow venation (below, left), the underside with dense hairs, and measuring 4-10 × 3-6 cm. Flowering takes place in March-April, the catkins (below, right, male) appearing before the leaves.—**Distribution:** Europe to north-eastern Asia. Native to Britain, where it grows abundantly particularly in damp places.

# Purple Willow  *Salix purpurea*

**Characteristics:** usually a shrub up to 3 m in height, rarely a slender tree to 10 m. The shoots are a shiny purple to greenish-brown or grey. The leaves are lanceolate to linear-lanceolate, often broader at the tip and measuring c. 10 × 1.2 cm. The buds are often opposite (fig. 59). The stamens of the male catkins (above, left) are at first reddish, whereas in other species they are usually bright yellow.—**Distribution:** central and southern Europe. Used in basket-making. Also known as Purple Osier.

# Eared Sallow  *Salix aurita*

**Characteristics:** usually a shrub not exceeding 2 m in height. The leaves which measure 2-4 × 1-2 cm, are ovate, the upperside wrinkled, the underside showing conspicuous venation, and the tips recurved. Female catkin as in the illustration above, right. Usually growing in non-calcareous soil, often in damp woodland.

# Common Osier  *Salix viminalis*

**Characteristics:** the strikingly long shoots (below, left) bear leaves that are usually ten times as long as they are wide. The undersides of the leaves have silky white hairs growing parallel to the venation. Grows in damp, rich soils, particularly near to rivers and lakes, and frequently cultivated for basketry.

# Dark-leaved Willow  *Salix nigricans*

**Characteristics:** grows to a height of c. 4 m. The leaves are dark green above, grey to blue-green below, but the tip is usually pure green; they become black when dried. As in all willows the seeds (below, right) are hairy and this helps in their dispersal by wind. Grows mainly in damp soils.

# Hornbeam *Carpinus betulus*

**Characteristics:** a tree up to c. 25 m in height (above, left), which is much planted as a hedge because the leaves often remain on the plant until the following spring. The crown is broad and round or irregularly ovate, sometimes conical. The bole may show deep fluting. The bark is grey to silvery-grey, with smooth patches separated by dark, irregular fissures. The leaves are alternate, ovate to longish-ovate (above, right), rounded to heart-shaped at the base and measuring 5-11 × 4-6 cm; they have 15 pairs of parallel, unbranched veins and their edges are double-toothed. The foliage is golden-yellow in autumn, more brownish in winter. The buds are spindle-shaped, about 1 cm long (fig. 60), and red-brown to greenish-brown. The tree flowers in April-May, sometimes earlier. The male flowers are on the previous year's growth, the female flowers on the new growth (below, left). The fruits develop in a cluster 6 cm long with c. 8 pairs of nutlets. Each pair is close to a green bract which is 3-4 cm long (below, right).—**Distribution:** Europe, from the Pyrenees eastwards to Asia Minor. A native tree in south-eastern England, and planted in other parts of the country.

The tree seldom lives for more than 150 years and is often starting to die back at 100 years. The shoots usually continue to grow up to autumn, so young leaves can still be seen at the tips. The hard timber is used for making mallets, wooden balls and rollers, and provides a good heating fuel.

The Hornbeam belongs to the Birch family which includes Silver Birch, Alder and Hazel.

# Common Hazel  *Corylus avellana*

**Characteristics:** usually a bushy shrub with dense foliage, rarely growing as a small tree up to c. 5 m in height, sometimes more. The bark is shiny brown to grey-brown, becoming slightly scaly or later ridged. The leaves are ovate or roundish and pointed with the base usually heart-shaped (above, left and fig. 39), and the petioles hairy. The pale brown shoots are covered with long, stiff hairs. The buds are ovate and reddish to greenish (fig. 61). Flowering is in February-April, before the leaves appear. The brownish-yellow male catkins, 3-6 cm long and shaped like little sausages, appear in autumn and open usually in February when they become pale yellow. The female flowers are ovate structures, 3-5 mm long, from which the red styles protrude (above, right, above the male catkins). The fruits are tasty, nutritious nuts, enclosed in a hard casing (below) which are much appreciated by squirrels, Jays, woodpeckers, mice and dormice. The nuts have a diameter of 1.5-2.0 cm and grow in clusters of four or more, each partially enclosed in two green bracts which are deeply toothed.—**Distribution:** throughout Europe to 68°N and in Asia Minor. A native plant in Britain where it mainly grows on chalk and limestone soils in areas with sufficient precipitation, and extending up to altitudes of 1,800 m in the mountains. Some varieties are cultivated, the nuts being a valuable crop.

# Birches  *Betula*

Trees or shrubs with buds arranged spirally and leaves that never have entire margins. Male and female flowers are on the same tree, the males as cylindrical catkins which appear as the leaves open, the female flowers in catkins or clusters at the ends of short side branches. When ripe the fruiting catkins break up and release numerous small winged nutlets. There are about 40 species of birch in Europe, temperate Asia and North America. They will grow rapidly in poor soil provided there is plenty of light.

# Downy or White Birch  *Betula pubescens*

**Characteristics:** a tree usually not more than 20 m in height. The twigs, which are stiff, grow upwards, not pendant. The tree is often attacked by a type of fungus which causes the production of galls known as witches' brooms (opposite). Young shoots are greyish-purple and hairy, without warts. The bark is at first red-brown, later becoming white to greyish-white with horizontal grey or brown bands. The leaves are 3-5 cm long, almost circular with rounded lateral corners, a short pointed tip, and a rounded base which is sometimes slightly heart-shaped. The leaf margins are double-toothed, i.e. the larger teeth are themselves toothed. The petiole has dense, soft hairs. The buds (fig. 62) are ovate to longish-ovate, often standing off from the stem. One-year old twigs are hairy, with few or no wax glands. Flowering takes place in April-May, the fruiting catkins usually being pendant.—**Distribution:** Europe and northern Asia, on damp moors and heathland, with good light. A native tree in Britain and particularly common in the Scottish Highlands.

In spring the leaves have a delicate scent. The timber is hard and used for furniture, plywood and as a fuel.

# Silver Birch *Betula pendula*

**Characteristics:** a tree up to 30 m in height (above, left). The crown is at first narrow, pointed and conical with upward-growing branches, but it gradually becomes more dome-shaped with long, pendant branches. Young shoots are sticky, with rough, white warts. The bark is at first reddish-brown, later pinkish with patches of scales, and finally silvery with large black diamonds. The base is often much fissured. The buds are very similar to those of the preceding species. The leaves are triangular with a distinct point, the lateral corners not or scarcely rounded, the base broadly wedge-shaped or truncated, the margin double-toothed and the leaf blade smooth, not hairy. Flowering takes place in April-May, with the male catkins as shown (above, right). The female catkins, which are about 1.5 cm long, are at the base of the male catkins. They are ripe by late autumn when they break up, releasing the seeds.—**Distribution:** Europe and Asia Minor. A native tree in Britain, growing particularly on heathland and hills with light soils, and often planted in towns where the soil is not too alkaline.

# Dwarf Birch *Betula nana*

**Characteristics:** a low-growing to creeping shrub up to 50 cm in height, rarely to 1 m. The young shoots are brown with dense hairs, but without warts. The leaves are 5-15 mm long, and roundish with coarse teeth, but not pointed. Flowering takes place in April-June, the catkins being erect (below, left).—**Distribution:** central and northern Europe and North America, on high moorland. This plant is also abundant in the ice-free parts of Greenland.

## *Betula humilis*

**Characteristics:** a shrub 50-200 cm in height, with blackish-brown to brown bark. The shoots have large, pale yellow, resinous warts. The leaves are 1.5-3.0 cm long, rounded-ovate, toothed and smooth with 4-5 pairs of veins.

Flowering takes place in April-May, with erect fruiting catkins (below, right).—**Distribution:** central and northern Europe, western Asia, on moors and heaths.

# Alders *Alnus*

Trees or shrubs with spirally arranged leaves and stalked buds (except in *Alnus viridis*). A cross section of a shoot shows a triangular core. The male and female flowers are on the same tree and are pollinated by wind. Flowering is in March-April, the male flowers long and cylindrical, appearing before the leaves, the females shorter, usually several together, ripening to ovoid "cones", which remain on the tree long after the seeds have been shed (above, right).

# Common Alder *Alnus glutinosa*

**Characteristics:** a tree up to 22 m in height, often with several main stems, the crown rather loose, and at first conical. The shoots are sticky, hence the specific name. The bark is at first purplish-brown, later becoming blackish-grey to dark brown and fissured. The leaves (below) are roundish to broadly ovate, 4-10 cm long, toothed and with 5-6 pairs of veins. They are sticky when young and the underside is usually rust-coloured and hairy. The buds are longish-ovate, brown to violet-red (fig. 64). Female catkins with a distinct stalk, as also in the male catkins (above, left). The seeds are usually dispersed by water.—**Distribution:** Europe to the Caucasus and Siberia, also north-western Africa, mainly along the banks of rivers and in other damp places. Native to Britain. Alders do not usually live for more than 120 years. The timber turns a deep yellowish-brown colour on exposure to air and when dried is brownish-red.

The Green Alder (*A. viridis*) is usually a shrub c. 3 m in height with smooth, dark brown bark. The leaves have 7-10 pairs of nerves and the buds are sessile (fig. 65). European mountains: introduced into Britain.

The Grey Alder (*A. incana*) is a tree up to 25 m in height, with smooth, silvery to dark grey bark and leaves with 9-15 pairs of veins. The buds are similar to those of the Common Alder, but hairy. Europe, Caucasus, up to altitudes of 1,600 m. There are several varieties. Introduced into Britain.

# Common Beech  *Fagus sylvatica*

**Characteristics:** a tree up to 30 or even 40 m in height with a spread of up to 6 m (above, left); large specimens have no branches for 15-20 m above the ground. The crown is at first conical, later more domed and much branched. The trunk is smooth with silvery-grey to ash-grey bark. The leaves (above, right) are ovate to elliptical, rounded at the base, 4-10 × 3-7 cm, the margin wavy or slightly toothed, with 5-9 veins on each side. The leaf upperside is dark green (pale green when very new) and shiny, the underside at first silky. In autumn the foliage becomes yellow, pale brown, yellow-brown and later red-brown. The buds are long and spindle-shaped (fig. 67), standing off from the shoots. Flowering is in April-May, the male flowers in almost spherical, long-stalked bunches, the female on shorter stalks in the upper leaf axils (below, left). The fruit is the well-known beechmast, usually with two seeds in a soft-spined case (below, right).—**Distribution:** Europe, except in northern Scandinavia. A native in central and south-eastern England, and commonly planted in woodland and parks. In some places Beech is planted as a garden hedge. There are several selected varieties, including the Copper Beech which has dark purple leaves, and also a weeping form.

In general, Beeches grow best in a soil with sufficient humus and minerals, but they do not tolerate waterlogged ground. The seeds yield an edible oil and the reddish timber is used in furniture making.

Beech trees have a life span of about 300 years, but at 120-160 years most are starting to decay.

# Oaks  *Quercus* species

Trees up to about 45 m in height, with deeply fissured bark. A cross section of a twig shows a star-shaped core (fig. 68). The buds are ovate, somewhat rounded with several together at the tips of the shoots (fig. 69), and each has several scales. The flowers, which are wind-pollinated, appear in April-May. Male flowers are in hanging catkins, female flowers singly or several together. The fruit is an acorn held in a woody cup. The timber is very valuable.

# English Oak  *Quercus robur*

**Characteristics:** the trunk usually starts to branch fairly low down, giving a wide, domed crown (above). The leaves are irregularly lobed (fig. 45), the petiole being green and 3-8 mm long. The female flowers and the fruits have long stalks (below, left).—**Distribution:** Europe, including Britain, where it is most abundant in the lowlands.

# Sessile or Durmast Oak  *Quercus petraea*

**Characteristics:** the trunk is usually straight. The leaves mostly have symmetrical lobes, and a yellowish petiole, 1-3 cm long. The flowers and acorns are sessile or almost sessile (below, right).—**Distribution:** Europe and western Asia. Native to Britain where it is most abundant in the north and west.

The Turkey Oak (*Q. cerris*), originally from southern Europe and south-western Asia, is now quite commonly planted in Britain. The leaves mostly have 4-9 short, pointed lobes (fig. 46).

The Downy Oak (*Q. pubescens*) from southern Europe and Western Asia has downy twigs and leaves, the latter with 4-8 pairs of lobes (fig. 47).

The Red Oak (*Q. rubra*), an introduction from North America, has leaves up to 22 cm long and 4-8 pairs of deeply separated lobes (fig. 48). They turn orange to scarlet or brown in autumn. This is a fast-growing and valuable tree for woodland and parks.

# Common Walnut  *Juglans regia*

**Characteristics:** a tree up to 20-25 m in height, with a broad, spreading crown (above, left). The bark is silvery-grey, becoming deeply fissured. The leaves are 30-40 cm long with 5-9 (rarely up to 13) longish-elliptical leaflets; the margins are mostly untoothed, except in some of the very small leaflets. When rubbed the leaves give off a strong aromatic scent. The buds are broad and squat, greenish-grey to downy-grey (fig. 70). The flowers, which are wind-pollinated, appear in May. The male flowers are in short, cylindrical hanging catkins (below, left), the female flowers, usually 2-5 together, are at the ends of the shoots (below, right). The fruits are at first fleshy and green, later brown (above, right), and the ripe walnuts are 3-5 cm long.—**Distribution:** south-eastern Europe and eastwards to China. Introduced into Britain and western Europe at an early date. It thrives in warm, sunny places, with a deep rich soil and protection from late frosts, and in some districts grows up to altitudes of over 700 m. Walnuts are much planted as specimen trees in gardens and parks. The fruits are, of course, much appreciated, and the timber is extremely valuable.

# Elms  *Ulmus*

Trees up to 40 m in height, with striking asymmetrical, variable leaves, which are alternate and usually double-toothed. The inconspicuous flowers, which are wind-pollinated, appear in May. The fruits are flat nutlets surrounded by a membranous wing. Elms may live some hundreds of years. Since 1918 they have been threatened by Dutch Elm disease caused by the fungus *Graphium ulmi* which is transmitted by a beetle, and in Britain alone, perhaps millions have died in recent years.

# Smooth-leaved Elm  *Ulmus carpinifolia*

**Characteristics:** the young shoots are downy. The leaves (above) are shiny green above, usually with 8-12 pairs of veins, and measure 10 × 5 cm. The leaf buds are pointed and ovate, the flower buds roundish (fig. 71). The fruit is enclosed in an elliptical to ovate membrane, with a distal notch (fig. 37).—**Distribution:** Europe, south-west Asia and north-western Africa. This species may be native to south-eastern England, but opinions differ and it is more probable that it was introduced a long time ago.

In the Wych Elm (*U. glabra*) the leaves are asymmetrical and even broader than in fig. 35. They are 8-16 cm long, with 16-20 pairs of veins, the upperside very rough due to stiff hairs. The buds are squat and reddish-brown (fig. 72). The fruit is a nutlet in the centre of a winged membrane.—**Distribution:** northern and central Europe, western Asia. A native tree in Britain, where it is most abundant in the north and west.

Dutch Elm, known botanically as *Ulmus × hollandica*, consists of a number of hybrids between *U. carpinifolia* and *U. glabra*. Probably introduced into Britain in the 17th century.

The European White Elm (*U. laevis*) has hairy shoots. The leaves are similar in shape to those of the Wych Elm but the upperside is not rough. The buds are pointed and ovate, and the edges of the fruits are fringed (fig. 36).—**Distribution:** central Europe to western Asia. Rarely planted in Britain.

# Mistletoe  *Viscum album*

**Characteristics:** an evergreen shrub up to about 1 m in height, growing on trees. The shoots and leaves are rather pale greenish, the latter being opposite, leathery, 3-5 cm long, lanceolate, becoming narrower towards the base, with only a short stalk. The yellowish flowers, which have tiny petals, appear in March to April, the males and females being on separate plants. The fruit is a white or yellowish berry about the size of a pea (below, right) with a single seed surrounded by very glutinous pulp; it ripens during the winter. Mistletoe is a parasite deriving some of its nutrient from the host tree.—**Distribution:** throughout temperate Europe. It is common in southern and particularly western England, except Cornwall, but does not occur in Scotland or Ireland. Mistletoe is mostly seen growing on deciduous trees, especially apples, poplars, pears, hazels and various cherries, but rarely on oaks or on conifers.

Mistletoe seeds are normally disseminated by birds. The layer of sticky pulp prevents the bird from swallowing the seed when eating the berry. Instead it scrapes the seed off its beak on to a branch, where it adheres and later germinates. Owing to its unusual growth habits the plant was at one time thought to have magical properties and it played a part in the myths of the ancient Greeks.

The much rarer *Loranthus europaeus* is a branched deciduous shrub with dark brown to blackish-grey shoots. The leaves are dark green with a distinct stalk. The fruits are pale yellow berries. This plant, which occurs in Europe but not in Britain, grows as a parasite on the young wood only of trees, mainly oaks and Sweet Chestnut.

# Traveller's Joy  *Clematis vitalba*

**Characteristics:** a climbing plant growing up to a height of 7 m and more, with woody stems. The leaves are opposite, with 3-5 ovate to heart-shaped, entire or toothed, stalked leaflets each 3-10 cm long. The whole leaf is 25 cm or more in length (fig. 19). The stalks of the leaves and leaflets are prehensile and they twine round branches as the plant climbs, thus providing support. The buds are cone-shaped and covered with dense down (fig. 74). The flowers (above) appear in June-September in clusters growing from the axils of the upper leaves, or at the tips of the shoots. There are no true petals, their function being taken over by 4-5 sepals which are yellowish-green outside, white inside. The sepals surround a number of yellow stamens and carpels. After flowering the styles elongate into long feathery structures (awns) which with their attached seeds may remain on the plant until the following spring (below); these attractive structures which help in distributing the seeds by wind, give this plant its alternative name of Old Man's Beard.—**Distribution:** mainly central and southern Europe. An abundant plant in southern England, particularly on calcareous soils.

There are several other species of *Clematis* in Europe. These include Fragrant Clematis (*C. flammula*) from southern Europe, which has very fragrant white flowers, and the slender *C. viticella*, also from southern Europe, with fragrant purple flowers. In addition there are, of course, numerous widely distributed cultivated varieties.

# Common Barberry  *Berberis vulgaris*

**Characteristics:** a deciduous shrub up to 3 m in height with ribbed stems which are greenish in the first year, later brownish, then whitish-grey. The leaves are ovate to longish-ovate, 3-6 cm long and sharply toothed on short shoots; there are three sharp spines at each node. The buds are as shown in fig. 75. The yellow flowers, which are insect-pollinated, appear in May-June in hanging clusters 5-7 cm long. The fruits are ovate to longish, and bright red, rarely yellow.—**Distribution:** Europe northwards to about latitude 60°N, and eastwards to the Caucasus and Anatolia. Found in many parts of Britain. In the wild this shrub is found on sunny, rocky slopes, in open woodland, along the edges of woodland, particularly in limestone areas. Under favourable conditions it can form dense thickets, which provide ideal nest sites for small birds.

The fruits are edible and can be made into a palatable jam. Common Barberry is a host plant of the disease known as wheat rust and so has been exterminated in some areas. The plant should not be confused in winter with Gooseberry (*Ribes uva-crispa*), another thorny plant, up to 1 m in height, with three- or five-lobed leaves, and pointed, longish-ovate buds (fig. 16).

# Common Pear  *Pyrus communis*

**Characteristics:** a tree up to about 20 m in height, with a tall, conical crown, which is narrow when young. The bark is dark brown to blackish, becoming deeply fissured. The branches have numerous smooth or slightly hairy short shoots, often with thorns. The leaves are ovate to roundish, 2-8 cm long, pointed and toothed; they are at first hairy, but soon become smooth, the upperside being shiny green, the underside paler. The buds are longish-ovate, pointed and dark brown, the scales often with ash-grey markings (fig. 78). The flowers, which appear in April-May before the leaves emerge, are about 3 cm across, with red stamens; they are illustrated on p. 77 (above). The fruits are pear-shaped to roundish, 2.5-5 cm long, becoming yellowish-green, very acid but later mellow and then edible.—**Distribution:** Europe and western Asia. Common in Britain, but it is doubtful whether truly native. Pear trees grow best in deep soil with a good content of minerals.

The dense hard timber is much valued and is used, among other things, in wood engraving, where it is second only to Box. Most of the trees seen in the wild are escapes from cultivation. There are, of course, numerous cultivated varieties which differ from one another in the shape, colour and flavour of the fruits.

# Crab Apple  *Malus sylvestris*

(fig. above is Common Pear, text p. 74)

**Characteristics:** a much branched shrub or tree up to 10 m in height, the shoots often thorny. The crown is roundish and broader than high. The bark is dark grey-brown, becoming deeply fissured. The leaves are pointed-ovate to roundish-ovate, on the average 3-5 × 2-4 cm, toothed and shiny, at least on the upperside, with usually only four pairs of prominent veins (fig. 53). The petiole is half the length of the leaf. The buds are downy (fig. 79), particularly those on short shoots. The flowers, which appear in April-May, are about 4 cm across, white or pale pink, with yellow stamens (below). The fruit is roundish, about 2-4 cm across, acid, the stalk shorter than the fruit, but longer than in the cultivated varieties.—**Distribution:** Europe and south-western Asia. Native to Britain, where in some areas it is quite common along the edges of woodland or in hedgerows. However, many such trees may be seedlings derived from cultivated varieties.

There are several other species of Crab Apple, many of which are widely cultivated as ornamental trees. For instance, the Siberian Crab (*M. baccata*) from northern China and Manchuria is a small tree with lanceolate leaves which produces numerous small white flowers in May.

# Whitebeam  *Sorbus aria*

**Characteristics:** a tree up to 12 m in height, or a shrub, often with several stems. The leaves are broadly elliptical to ovate, with 10-14 pairs of veins (above), toothed, the underside with dense white down. The buds are large, ovate or wedge-shaped, the scales green with a pale brown margin, fringed with white down (fig. 81). The white to pale yellowish-white flowers appear in May-June in clusters. The fruits are orange to scarlet berries.—**Distribution:** central and southern Europe. A native tree in many parts of southern England on chalky or sandy soils, and frequently planted in gardens and roadsides.

The Swedish Whitebeam (*S. intermedia*) grows to a height of about 10 m. Its leaves are broadly ovate to elliptical with 5-8 pairs of veins and distinctly lobed, the underside with white or greyish down. The fruits are ovate berries which are orange-red when ripe (below, left).—**Distribution:** Sweden and states bordering the Baltic. Planted in Britain, mainly in parks and streets.

# Wild Service Tree  *Sorbus torminalis*

**Characteristics:** a tree usually up to 15 m in height, sometimes more, with a crown that is at first conical, later high-domed. Trees with a trunk 1.80 m in circumference are up to 100 years old. The bark is ash-grey, smooth, breaking into scaly plates and then gradually becoming dark. The leaves are broadly ovate and lobed, up to about 10 × 10 cm (below, right and fig. 49), turning yellow in autumn. The buds are globular and shiny green (fig. 80). The flowers appear in loose clusters in May-June, each flower being 12 mm across. The fruits are ovate and brownish with pale speckles.—**Distribution:** Europe eastwards to the Caucasus and Syria, also in parts of northern Africa. A native tree in most parts of England.

# Rowan or Mountain Ash
## *Sorbus aucuparia*

**Characteristics:** a tree up to 15 m in height, often with several stems and seldom exceeding an age of 80 years. The crown is somewhat irregular but fairly broad. The bark is at first pale grey and smooth, then grey-brown with shallow grooves and scaly plates. The shoots are at first downy, then smooth and brown. The leaves are pinnate, up to 20 cm long, with 9-15 longish-elliptical, toothed leaflets, each 2-6 cm long (above); they turn yellow in autumn. The buds are downy (fig. 82). The white flowers (above) appear in May-June; they have a strong scent. The fruits are bright red berries about 1 cm across (below).—**Distribution:** everywhere in Europe, also North Africa and Asia Minor. A native tree in all areas, growing up to altitudes of nearly 1,000 m in Scotland. Commonly planted in streets and parks, for this is an undemanding tree as regards soil type, but it does require good light. The bitter fruits can be made into an excellent jelly for eating with meat and game, and they are also enjoyed by birds.

The name Mountain Ash is misleading as the tree is not related to the Common Ash. There are a few varieties of Rowan, one of which has orange-yellow berries.

The True Service Tree (*S. domestica*) is a tree up to 20 m in height with rough bark, and pinnate leaves 15-20 cm long with 11-21 longish-elliptical, sharply toothed leaves, each 3-8 cm long. The buds are ovate to longish-ovate, the scales green with brown edges (fig. 83), sticky and shiny. The cream-coloured flowers appear in May-June in terminal clusters. The fruits are pear-shaped to globular, 1-3 cm in diameter, greenish to brownish, reddening on the sunny side, sour and edible.—**Distribution:** southern Europe and western Asia. Not native to Britain, where it has been planted in a few places. It is very slow-growing and is said to have a life span of up to 600 years.

# Midland Hawthorn
*Crataegus oxyacanthoides*

Also known as *C. laevigata*.—**Characteristics:** a shrub or small tree up to 2-5 m in height; at an age of 500 years it may reach a height of 12 m and a trunk girth of 4 m. As a tree it may have branches almost down to the ground. The shoots often have thorns up to 15 cm long. The bark is at first pale grey and smooth, becoming brown and fissured. The leaves vary in shape, but most are roughly ovate with three to five pairs of toothed lobes, and with toothed stipules (fig. 14). The buds are ovate to globular, reddish to red-brown, in ones or twos below the thorns (fig. 84). The white, scented flowers appear in May-June in dense clusters (above). The fruits are ovate to spherical berries, about 1 cm across, and scarlet (below, left), usually containing 2 seeds.—**Distribution:** Europe from southern Scandinavia to the Urals, Asia Minor and northwestern Africa. In Britain, growing mainly in southern England.

The Hawthorn or Quickthorn (*C. monogyna*) is a similar plant in which the leaves are more deeply incised (fig. 15) and the flowers have only one style, whereas in the Midland Hawthorn there are two. The berries have only one seed. Found throughout Europe and east to Afghanistan; this is much the commonest hawthorn in Britain.

# Medlar  *Mespilus germanica*

**Characteristics:** a small tree up to 6 m in height. The leaves are longish-lanceolate to longish-ovate, 6-12 cm long, with entire wavy margins, dark yellow-green above, paler with dense down below. The white flowers, 4-6 cm across, appear singly in May-June. The fruits (below, right) are globose, about the size of a walnut, with persistent sepals, becoming brown and containing five seeds.—**Distribution:** originally southern Europe. Planted in some gardens in Britain, but not very commonly. The fruit is edible when soft or bletted.

# Dewberry *Rubus caesius*

**Characteristics:** a scrambling shrub, the shoots armed with small prickles, usually found growing over other shrubs. The leaves have three leaflets (fig. 12), the two lateral leaflets almost sessile (above). The buds are longish-ovate, greenish to reddish, usually with fine hairs, particularly at the tip (fig. 85). The whitish flowers appear in May-September in small, loose clusters (above). The fruits which are bluish with a waxy bloom have few, but relatively large segments (below, left).—**Distribution:** Europe and western Asia. A common plant in Britain.

The very similar and much commoner Bramble or Blackberry, *R. fruticosus*, has the same distribution. It, too, has long scrambling shoots armed with numerous powerful, but easily detached thorns. The leaves are prickly with 3-5 leaflets. The white or pink flowers appear in May-November. The fruits are reddish at first, and purplish-black when ripe. There are hundreds of varieties of this ubiquitous plant.


# Raspberry *Rubus idaeus*

**Characteristics:** an erect, perennial shrub, growing to a height of 1 m or rather more, the stems armed with weak prickles. The leaves have 3-7 leaflets, the underside usually with whitish down (below, right). The white flowers appear in May-August in long clusters at the ends of the side branches. The fruit (below, right) is pink to red, separating easily from the base when ripe.—**Distribution:** Europe and western Asia. A common plant in Britain, in some places as an escape from cultivation.

# Snowy Mespilus  *Amelanchier ovalis*

**Characteristics:** a shrub up to 3 m in height, usually less, producing runners. Shoots are at first downy, then smooth, dark brown. The leaves are ovate to roundish-ovate, at first with white down on the underside, slightly toothed or notched; they measure 2-4 × 2-3.5 cm. The buds have a white down, and at least the terminal bud is spindle-shaped, the scales finely fringed (fig. 86). Flowering takes place in April-May with 3-10 flowers in an erect open cluster (above, left). The flower segments are broadly lanceolate. The fruits (above, right) are dark blue to black, spherical, 1 cm in diameter, and with a pleasant to insipid taste.—**Distribution:** Europe and north-western Africa, in the mountains up to altitudes of about 2,000 m. This is a lime-loving plant growing naturally on cliffs and rocky slopes, where it makes an attractive sight when flowering in spring. It is quite commonly planted in gardens.

# Mountain Avens  *Dryas octopetala*

**Characteristics:** a small, evergreen shrub, 6-12 cm in height, with a short, prostrate or creeping stem and numerous branches. It has been estimated that a plant with a stem only 8.5 mm in diameter may be up to 90 years old. The leaves are longish-ovate to longish-elliptical (fig. 40), coarsely notched, the upperside deep green, the underside with silvery-white down; they have a length of 1-3 cm. The petiole has a fringe of hairs. Flowering takes place in May-August. The rather large, white, anemone-like flowers (below) are about 3 cm across. The calyx and the flower stalk are downy, the latter being about 5-20 cm long. The fruits have long feathery awns or tails.—**Distribution:** Europe, northern Asia, Greenland and North America, on high mountains or in Arctic regions. A fairly common plant in the limestone mountain areas in northern England, parts of Ireland, and particularly in northern Scotland.

# Wild Rose  *Rosa* species

There are several wild rose species in Europe and numerous hybrids which often renders identification difficult. Only one representative species is described here. All are erect or climbing shrubs (above, left). The shoots may grow up to a height of 5 m into the crown of a tree. The stems have sharp, curved prickles or thorns, which are easily detached. The leaves are pinnate with leaf-like stipules at the base of the petiole (fig. 13). The buds are ovate to almost cylindrical, and smooth (fig. 87). Flowering takes place in June-July, the flowers being usually white to red and fragrant. The fruits, known as hips or heps, are typical of the genus. They are roundish-ovate or globular and they contain numerous seeds surrounded by a kind of pulp.

# Dog Rose  *Rosa canina*

**Characteristics:** a shrub up to 3 m in height with arched, overhanging stems, which have large, hooked prickles. The leaves have 5-7 ovate to elliptical leaflets, each 2-4 cm long, the margins entire or double-toothed. The flowers (above, right) are pink to white, 4-5 cm across, with lanceolate sepals which have feathery edges. After flowering, the sepals turn back and fall off before the 2-3 cm long hips become red (below).—**Distribution:** Europe up to latitudes 62°N and temperate Asia. An abundant plant in Britain, particularly in hedgerows and thickets.

# Cherries and Plums  *Prunus* species

Trees or shrubs with spirally arranged leaves which have toothed margins and stipules. The flowers, which are pollinated by insects, usually have 5 petals and 5 sepals. The fruits contain a single stone.

# Bird Cherry  *Prunus padus*

**Characteristics:** a tree up to 15 m in height with a dense crown or a shorter shrub with overhanging branches. The bark is blackish-grey, later developing shallow fissures. The leaves are ovate or elliptical with a short point, finely toothed, slightly cordate at the base, 6-12 cm long, turning yellowish-red in autumn. The buds are long and pointed, the tips usually turn inwards (fig. 88). Flowering takes place in April-June. The flowers appear in loose, often drooping racemes (above and below, left) and they have a very strong scent. The fruit is about the size of a pea, deep black and with a bitter taste (below, right). The stone is oval, wrinkled and much eaten by birds.—**Distribution:** Europe and temperate Asia. Locally distributed in Britain, but not as a wild plant in southern England. It grows mostly in woodland, hedgerows and thickets, but not in alkaline soils.

The Black or Rum Cherry (*Prunus serotina*) is a tree up to 35 m in height. The undersides of the leaves have rust-brown hairs along the midribs. The flowers appear in May and the fruit is oval, dark purple and bitter with a smooth stone. Introduced from North America for its fine timber and planted in woodland, parks and gardens.

# Wild Cherry or Gean  *Prunus avium*

**Characteristics:** a tree up to about 20 m in height, sometimes reaching 30 m, and rarely living for more than 90 years. The crown is broadly conical, the branches thick with numerous short shoots which carry the leaves in dense clusters. The bark is reddish-brown to grey, shiny, with circular, horizontal colour stripes and a tendency to be shed, eventually becoming dark with shallow fissures. The leaves are usually ovate or longish-ovate, pointed and measuring up to 15 × 7 cm. The undersides of the leaves only have hairs on the veins, and the leaf margin usually has glands (fig. 51). The petiole normally has 1-2 red glands (fig. 50). In autumn the foliage turns bright orange to red. The buds are ovate and pointed, pale brown, with numerous small scales (fig. 89). The flowers appear in April-May, in bunches of two or more (above, left). The fruit is red or black, globular and usually sweet.—**Distribution:** Europe and temperate Asia. Widely distributed in England, southern Scotland and Ireland in woods and hedgerows, and cultivated varieties are much planted in gardens and orchards.

# Sour Cherry  *Prunus cerasus*

**Characteristics:** a shrub or small tree, up to 10 m in height with a loose crown (below). The leaf margins are toothed with glands, but the petioles usually have no glands, or if present they are small and only at the leaf base. The leaves are ovate, narrowing at the base and almost always broadest in the middle. The branches are thin and often overhanging. The flowers appear in April-May, and the fruits are red and acid.—**Distribution:** originally south-eastern Europe and South-western Asia, but extensively cultivated for their fruits, known as Morellos (above, right).

*Prunus fruticosa* is a shrub up to 1 m in height with flowers similar to those of the Sour Cherry, but smaller. St Lucie's Cherry (*P. mahaleb*) is a small tree with overhanging branches and sour, pea-sized, black fruits.

# Sloe or Blackthorn  *Prunus spinosa*

**Characteristics:** a much branched, very spiny shrub with dark brown bark, up to about 4 m in height. The leaves are longish-elliptical to broad-lanceolate, finely toothed, measuring 2-5 × 1-2 cm (fig. 17). The buds are almost spherical, usually up to three above a leaf scar, of which the central ones are often and the lateral ones always flower buds. Flowering takes place in April-May, before the leaves appear. The flowers are up to 1.5 cm across, in dense clusters (above, left). Fruits are spherical, about 1 cm across and blackish-blue with a pale blue bloom (below), and like the flowers they are at the tips of spiny short shoots, which stick out almost at right angles from the long shoots. The plant produces numerous suckers giving a dense thicket.—**Distribution:** throughout Europe, except Iceland, and northern Asia, mostly in open woodland.

# Plum  *Prunus domestica*

**Characteristics:** a shrub or small tree, often thornless, with smooth branches and up to about 7 m in height. The leaves are longish-ovate to lanceolate, 5-10 cm long, finely toothed or notched. The petioles usually have 1-2 small glands. The buds are wedge-shaped, pointed, reddish-brown, on protruding bud "cushions" (fig. 91). Flowering is in April-May, usually before the leaves appear (above, right). The fruit is a smooth stone surrounded by fleshy pulp.—**Distribution:** originally from the Orient, this is probably a hybrid between Sloe and the Cherry Plum (*P. cerasifera*). There are numerous cultivated forms, including Greengages and Damsons.

# Locust Tree or False Acacia
*Robinia pseudacacia*

**Characteristics:** a tree up to 25 (30) m in height and a member of the pea family. The bole may have a circumference of 2.3 m or more. The crown is loose and open and the branches are twisting. In young trees the bark is smooth, but it soon becomes fissured like that of an oak. The shoots are greenish to dark red-brown, with a pair of short thorns near each bud (fig. 92) and on young suckers the spines may be up to 4 cm long. The leaves are alternate, pinnate, about 20 cm long, with 7-19 elliptical to ovate, entire leaflets, each 3-4 cm long, the rounded tips having a tiny spine which is a continuation of the central vein. The fragrant white flowers appear in June in closely packed racemes up to 20 cm long (above). The fruits are smooth pods, up to 11 cm long, which eventually turn dark reddish-brown (below). The buds for the following year are hidden in the petioles until the leaves fall in autumn. This tree produces numerous root suckers.—**Distribution:** originally eastern and mid-western United States, but introduced to Europe in the early 17th century, in fact in 1601 by the Paris nurseryman Robin. It came to Britain in the 1630s and is now abundant on light sandy and other soils in the gardens and parks of southern England, but less common in the north and in Scotland. This is one of the latest trees to come into leaf in the spring. The flowers are much visited by honey-bees.

# Dyer's Greenweed *Genista tinctoria*

**Characteristics:** an erect shrub, 30-60 cm in height, with spirally arranged leaves, which are elliptical to lanceolate, 1-2.5 cm long, with entire margins. The flowers, which appear in June-July, are yellow, in short racemes 2-6 cm long (above, left).—**Distribution:** Europe and western Asia, and quite common in most of England, extending into southern Scotland. A yellow dye was at one time produced from this plant.

# Spiny Rest-harrow *Ononis spinosa*

**Characteristics:** a much-branched shrub about 30 cm in height, with sharp spines and large pink flowers 2 cm across (above, right) appearing in summer.—**Distribution:** Europe, including Britain but not Ireland, in badly cultivated land and waste ground.

# Wild Thyme *Thymus serpyllum*

**Characteristics:** a small, perennial sub-shrub, up to 10-30 cm in height with procumbent to erect, much branched stems (below). The short stems root at frequent intervals, eventually forming a mat. The very small leaves are opposite, somewhat rough, longish- or roundish-elliptical gradually merging with the petiole. They have oil glands which release a pleasant aromatic scent. The flowers are purple, rarely white, usually six in a whorl, several of which form an erect, leafy spike. There are numerous varieties of this species and also several other species of the genus *Thymus.*—**Distribution:** Europe and western Asia. A very abundant plant in Britain, growing mainly on banks and in dry, upland pastures. In the Himalayas it has been found at altitudes up to 4,500 m.

# Shrubby Milkwort  *Polygala chamaebuxus*

**Characteristics:** an evergreen, mainly creeping perennial shrub, growing to a height of 25 cm, and covering an area up to 50 cm across. The shoots are yellowish-green to reddish. The leaves, which are arranged spirally, are leathery, elliptical and lanceolate, pointed at the tips (figs. 41, 42). The flowers, which appear in April-May, are up to 1.5 cm long, usually yellow with purple tips, but may be pink, red or white (above). They appear in April-September.—**Distribution:** central Europe to Italy, in grassy areas and woods, also on mountains. Not native to Britain.

# Box  *Buxus sempervirens*

**Characteristics:** an evergreen shrub or small tree up to about 24 m in height. The leaves are opposite, ovate-elliptical, thick, shiny, about 1 cm long, usually broadest in their lower third, and showing 20 often indistinct veins on each side. The small, inconspicuous, yellow-green flowers appear in April-May, with several male and a few female flowers in a cluster at the base of the upper leaves (below, left, much enlarged). The fruit is a hard capsule (below, right), with three short stiff beaks, and containing two black seeds.—**Distribution:** Europe and northern Asia, mainly in rocky, limestone areas. Rare in Britain as a wild plant, but widely grown in gardens. There are several varieties. The timber is very fine-grained and much used for wood engraving.

# Holly   *Ilex aquifolium*

**Characteristics:** an evergreen shrub up to 6-8 m in height, or sometimes a tree several hundred years old and up to 16 m or more in height, with a pyramidal crown. The branches are dark to pale green and smooth. The leaves vary in shape on a single tree, although always leathery. Up to a height of very approximately 2 m they are ovate to elliptical, 3-8 cm long with 6-8 pairs of very sharp, yellowish spines. Further up on the tree the leaves are ovate, entire with only a single spine at the tip. The male and female flowers are on separate trees. These appear in May-June in the leaf axils and are white and fragrant. The fruits are almost spherical coral-red berries about the size of a pea. They usually remain on the plant over winter and are then eaten by birds; they mostly germinate about two years later. These attractive berries are poisonous to humans.—**Distribution:** western, central and southern Europe. A native plant throughout Britain, except in the Orkneys, Shetlands and Caithness. Holly grows well in most types of soil, but particularly in those with a content of calcium. It is often found growing wild in the semi-shade under Beech, also in hedges, and is commonly planted in gardens to provide shelter and an attractive show of berries. There are numerous cultivated varieties, including some with variegated foliage.

# Spindle-tree  *Euonymus europaeus*

**Characteristics:** a deciduous shrub, rarely a small tree, up to 6-7 m in height. The young twigs are green, warty, usually with four sides due to narrow corky ridges, more rarely roundish. The leaves are opposite, elliptical-lanceolate, 3-10 cm long and finely toothed (fig. 31), turning an attractive red in autumn. The buds are ovate (fig. 93). The small, inconspicuous yellow-green flowers appear in the leaf axils in May-June; they have four petals. The fruit is a small pink to bright red berry or capsule containing four white seeds each enclosed in an orange mantle or aril (opposite).
—**Distribution:** Europe, including Britain, and western Asia, up to altitudes of about 2,000 m, growing in hedges, along the edges of woodland, on rocky slopes and as an undershrub in open woodland. The hard, yellowish-white timber is used in turnery. The seeds, and also the leaves and bark, contain a bitter, poisonous substance which induces vomiting. However, birds eat the seeds without suffering. Black aphids (blackfly) lay their overwintering eggs on the buds.

The Broad-leaved Spindle-tree (*E. latifolius*) is very similar to the preceding species, but it differs in having long, pointed buds, greenish-red flowers, twigs without the corky ridges, and usually seed capsules with five lobes.

The Warty Spindle-tree (*E. verrucosus*) is a similar species from Eastern Europe which has rounded twigs with dark brown warts and green flowers marked with fine red dots. The fruit capsule is yellowish-red, with black seeds and an orange aril.

# Maples  *Acer*

Trees with opposite, long-stalked, usually lobed leaves, and inconspicuous flowers in terminal or axillary clusters. The fruits, each with two seeds, have membranous wings. The Latin name of the genus, meaning sharp or pointed, possibly refers to the tips of the leaf lobes. The flowers are much visited by honey-bees.

# Sycamore  *Acer pseudoplatanus*

**Characteristics:** a tree up to 40 m in height with a broad, domed crown (above). The bark is at first smooth and grey, later becoming brown and fissured, forming small square scales. The leaves (below, left) are up to 16 cm across, dark green above, grey-green below, usually with five lobes, the indentations pointed, the margins with uneven teeth. The bud scales are green with dark edges (fig. 94). The yellowish-green flowers, which appear in May-June after the leaves, have very short petals. The winged fruits, each about 3 cm long, are in bunches (below, right).—**Distribution:** central and southern Europe. Not native to Britain but probably introduced by the Romans, and now an abundant tree in many areas. Sycamores do best in deep soil, and require a moderate amount of light and warmth. They probably have a life span of up to 500 years, and a tree of this age may have a trunk diameter of 3-5 m.

# Norway Maple  *Acer platanoides*

**Characteristics:** a tree up to 30 m in height, with a dense, domed crown. The bark is smooth, reddish-grey, becoming blackish with longitudinal folds, but not scaling. The leaves (above, left and fig. 28) have five lobes with the teeth rather elongated and the indentations rounded, in autumn turning bright yellow, sometimes orange or scarlet. The buds (fig. 95) are dark red-brown and shiny, the lateral scales of the pointed, ovate, terminal buds with distinct keels. The yellow flowers appear in March-April, before the leaves. The fruits are yellow-green with the wings spread to form an almost straight line.—**Distribution:** Europe as far north as southern Norway and southern Sweden. Introduced into Britain in the late 17th century and now commonly seen in gardens and parks in southern England, less so in the north and in Scotland. An adaptable tree which is said to have a life-span of up to 150 years.

# Field Maple  *Acer campestre*

**Characteristics:** a deciduous tree up to 12 (rarely 20) m, but usually less. The crown is domed and dense, the shoots brown, with fine down near the tip. The bark is pale brown becoming grey-brown with wide fissures. The leaves, which measure about $7 \times 10$ cm, have 3-5 main lobes (above, right), the underside with soft down. The flowers appear in late April or May in small, erect heads. The fruits are yellow-green with horizontal wings (below).—**Distribution:** Europe, western Asia, north-west Africa, particularly on calcareous soils. A native tree in England, where it is common in the south. The timber is valued for turnery.

The Italian Maple (*A. opalus*), from central and southern Europe, has five-lobed leaves. The Montpellier Maple (*A. monspessulanum*) with three-lobed leaves (fig. 27) comes from southern Europe and western Asia. Both these species have been planted in gardens and parks in Britain.

# Horse Chestnut  *Aesculus hippocastanum*

**Characteristics:** a tree up to about 38 m in height with a large, high-domed crown (above, left) with numerous branches, the lower ones often hanging down. The bark is grey-brown, becoming darker and breaking into large scales. The leaves are opposite and about 25 cm long with 5-7 elliptical, toothed leaflets, which become narrower towards the base (fig. 24). They are at first somewhat hairy, and in autumn they turn yellow. The buds (fig. 97) are large and sticky, with strikingly large leaf scars. The flowers appear in May-June in handsome, erect panicles (above, right) 20-30 cm tall. They are white with yellow and red markings. The fruits are roundish capsules, up to 6 cm across, with soft spines, and they enclose 1-2 brown seeds, the popular "conkers" (below).
—**Distribution:** originally the Balkans, but now widely planted throughout Europe. Introduced into Britain in the early 17th century, and now commonly seen in parks, streets and large gardens. This is a fast-growing tree with a normal life-span of 120-150 years, although a few are over 300 years old.

The Red Horse Chestnut *Ae.* × *carnea* is a hybrid with *Ae. pavia* and it has leaves with five leaflets each up to 15 cm long, slightly sticky buds and dull red flowers: its fruits are not very spiny. *Ae. pavia* is the Red Buck-eye of south-eastern United States. Its leaves have five lanceolate-elliptical leaflets, dry buds, reddish flowers and spineless fruit capsules.

# Alder Buckthorn *Frangula alnus*

**Characteristics:** usually a shrub up to 2 m in height, more rarely a small tree up to 5 m. The twigs are grey to violet-brown, and at first hairy. The bark is smooth, grey-brown with white cork cells. The leaves are alternate, broad-elliptical, usually pointed, 3-7 cm long, with 9-12 pairs of veins and untoothed margins (fig. 43). The buds are pale brown and downy, without scales. The terminal bud is scarcely larger than the lateral buds (fig. 98). Flowering takes place in May-June. The greenish-white flowers are in clusters of 10-20. The fruit is a pea-sized berry, at first red, then black, containing three seeds (above).—**Distribution:** Europe, including Britain, and western Asia, growing in hedges and undergrowth. The bark has an unpleasant smell, and at one time a purgative tea was made from it and from the berries. Consumption of the fresh bark causes vomiting.

# Buckthorn *Rhamnus catharticus*

**Characteristics:** a deciduous shrub up to 3 m in height or a small tree up to 6 m, with a life span of 100 years. The shoots are thorny, the bark dark brown, smooth, but becoming slightly fissured with age. The leaves are opposite, broad-elliptical, about 3-7 cm long, the base sometimes slightly heart-shaped, finely toothed, with 3-5 curved veins (fig. 18). The buds are pointed, ovate and dark brown (fig. 99), the edges of the scales paler. The greenish flowers (below, left) appear in May-June, in clusters at the base of some of the upper leaves. The fruit is a black berry (below, right).—**Distribution:** Europe and western Asia. Not very common in England. Unlike the Alder Buckthorn this species usually grows in hedges and thickets on calcareous soils. The berries are poisonous, with a purgative action.

# Limes *Tilia*

Trees with alternate, heart-shaped, but often somewhat asymmetrical leaves, and a domed crown when free-standing. The flowers are in small groups with an attached leafy, membranous bract, each individual flower having five yellowish to yellowish-white petals and sepals. The fruits are spherical to ovate nutlets, each with 1-3 seeds. The flowers are scented and they are visited by honey-bees. The leaves are often sticky and shiny due to substances produced by aphids. The European limes will hybridize with one another. When the fruit clusters are ripe they drop off and the bracts help them to be dispersed by the wind. The timber, which is rather soft, is used in turnery and carving.

# Large-leaved Lime  *Tilia platyphyllos*

**Characteristics:** a tree up to 40 m in height (fig. p. 115). The shoots are dark reddish-brown and at first quite hairy. The leaves (fig. 34) are up to about $10 \times 8.5$ cm, rounded-ovate, the underside with pale hairs on the veins. The buds are ovate, greenish to reddish or yellow-brown. The flowers appear in groups of 2-5, often 3 (above), with a pale green bract. The fruits have five distinct ribs.—**Distribution:** Europe and western Asia. Thought to be a native tree in some limestone districts in England (southern Yorkshire, Wye Valley).

# Small-leaved Lime  *Tilia cordata*

**Characteristics:** a tree up to 30 m in height (fig. p. 114), with smooth branches. The leaves are almost circular, the base heart-shaped, usually not over 6-7 cm in length and rather more asymmetrical than in the preceding species. The underside has striking rust-brown hairs in the angles of the veins (below, left). The buds are similar to those of the Large-leaved Lime (fig. 100). The flowers appear in July, usually about 14 days later than in the preceding species. The fruits are roundish and thin-shelled (fig. 101).—**Distribution:** throughout most of Europe. A native tree in England and Wales as far north as the Lake Distlrict, and to be found parlticularly in limestone areas.

The Common Lime (*T.* × *europaea*) is a hybrid between the two preceding species. The shoots are green, often with a reddish tinge and the buds are reddish-brown. The leaves are broadly-ovate, cordate at the base, the underside smooth except for whitish hairy tufts in the axils of the main veins. The flowers appear in June-July, before those of the Small-leaved Lime. The fruits are roundish, and covered with felt-like down (below, right).

# Mezereon  *Daphne mezereum*

**Characteristics:** an erect, deciduous shrub up to 1 m in height, with smooth, lanceolate leaves in groups at the end of the twigs; the leaf margins are entire (fig. 44). The buds, often several together, are longish-ovate and pointed (fig. 102). The flowers (above, left), which appear in February-April, are pink to purple, rarely white, usually in groups of three along the shoots and very fragrant. The fruits are bright red, pea-sized, very poisonous berries (above, right).—**Distribution:** Europe and western Asia, in woodland on lime. In Britain, perhaps only truly native in southern England.

The related Spurge Laurel, *Daphne laureola*, is an evergreen shrub up to 1 m in height, with dark green, leathery, lanceolate leaves, slightly fragrant, yellowish-green flowers and black berries. It is found in southern and western Europe, including parts of Britain, mostly in open woodland.

# Sea Buckthorn  *Hippophaë rhamnoides*

**Characteristics:** a deciduous shrub or small tree up to 6-10 m in height. The brown twigs have short, thorny shoots with numerous tiny, bronze to silvery-grey scales. The leaves are alternate, narrow lanceolate, 80 × 5-8 mm and they and the buds (fig. 103) are also scaly. The very small, inconspicuous flowers, male and female on different plants, appear in April-May, before the leaves, and they are wind-pollinated. The fruits are almost spherical, measuring about 6-8 mm and bright orange (below).—**Distribution:** Europe and western Asia, growing in river beds in mountainous areas, and along the coasts. In Britain this plant is locally distributed along the sea coasts in southern and eastern England.

# Ivy  *Hedera helix*

**Characteristics:** an evergreen climber. In addition to normal roots in the ground Ivy has small root-like excrescences from the stems which enable it to attach itself to walls, trees and other substrates, thus helping it climb. These structures which are 6-8 mm long grow away from the light and towards the substrate. The stem, which is much branched, creeps along the ground or climbs up to heights of 20 m or more. There are records of many giant specimens of this plant which are thought to be up to 400 years old (in Italy perhaps 1,000 years) with a stem diameter of 1 m. Ivy very rarely grows as an erect, non-climbing tree up to 6 m in height. The leaves vary considerably in shape. On non-flowering, usually lower branches they are leathery, shiny dark green with whitish veins, 4-10 cm long and with 3-5 lobes (above, left). Flowering shoots, on the other hand, have ovate to lanceolate, pointed leaves, without lobes. Flowering usually takes place in September-October. The inconspicuous, yellowish-green flowers are in short clusters (above, right); they have five short petals. The fruits are smooth berries, about the size of a pea (below) with 3-5 seeds, which ripen in the following spring. When unripe the berries are reddish-violet, then dark brown and finally bluish-black to black (very rarely yellow); they are poisonous to humans.—**Distribution:** Europe, northern Africa and western Asia. A very common plant on forest trees, rocks and old buildings from the lowlands up to altitudes of 1,800 m. Ivy tolerates a considerable amount of shade and will grow in any kind of soil, but particularly well in limey ground. There are numerous cultivated varieties with a vast array of different leaf shapes and sizes.

# Dogwood *Cornus sanguinea*

**Characteristics:** a shrub up to 4-5 m in height, with brownish-green shoots which may turn red in late autumn and winter. The leaves are opposite, broadly ovate to elliptical, pointed, deep green above, paler below with 3-5 pairs of veins, and they turn red in autumn. The buds (fig. 104) are naked, that is without scales, and narrow wedge-shaped. The whitish flowers appear in May-June in terminal clusters (above, left). The fruit is a very bitter black berry (above, right). —**Distribution:** Europe and western Asia in hedges and among other shrubs. An abundant plant in southern England, becoming scarcer in the north.

# Cornelian Cherry *Cornus mas*

**Characteristics:** a deciduous shrub or small tree up to 8 m in height, with greenish twigs. The leaves are opposite and very similar to those of the preceding species, but with white downy hairs in the angles of the veins on the underside. The buds have fine hairs, those producing leaves being longish and pointed, whereas the flower buds are roundish (fig. 105). Flowering takes place in February-April, before the leaves appear. The flowers are yellow in small clusters (below, left). They often provide the first food for overwintering butterflies and moths, and they are also visited by bees. The fruits are bright red with a stone (below, right).—**Distribution:** central and southern Europe, western Asia, but not native to Britain, where it is, however, a favourite garden shrub.

# Rhododendrons *Rhododendron*

**Characteristics:** shrubs with funnel-shaped or bell-shaped flowers growing in clusters and appearing in June-July. In Europe they are typical of the Alps. They belong to the heath family.

## *Rhododendron hirsutum*

**Characteristics:** an evergreen shrub up to 1 m in height. The leaves are elliptical, leathery, 1-3 cm long, mainly smooth but with a fringed margin, the underside with reddish glands. The shoots have shaggy hairs, becoming smooth and paler with age. The flowers are pink, rarely white.—**Distribution:** up to altitudes of 2,400 m in the Alps, where it is fully protected.

## *Rhododendron ferrugineum*

**Characteristics:** a shrub up to 2 m in height, often procumbent. The shoots are densely covered with rust-coloured scales. The leaves are elliptical to longish-lanceolate, the upperside smooth, the underside with dense rust-coloured scales. The flowers are dark pink, but otherwise very similar to those of the preceding species.—**Distribution:** Europe, in the Alps, Pyrenees, Appenines and in various parts of the Balkans.

# Bilberries, Whortleberries *Vaccinium*

Low-growing shrubs with alternate, short-stalked leaves, 1-3 cm long. The flowers are shaped like a bell. The fruits are berries containing several seeds and with persistent sepals. All the species are lime-haters.

## Red Whortleberry *Vaccinium vitis-idaea*

**Characteristics:** a small, evergreen, creeping shrub, 10-30 cm in height (above, left). The leaves are ovate, leathery, the underside with dark dots. The white or pinkish flowers appear in short, dense terminal clusters in May-June, and there may be a second flowering on the lower branches in August-October. The fruits are red and bitter.—**Distribution:** Europe, northern Asia, up to altitudes of 3,000 m. Also known as Cowberry.

## Bilberry *Vaccinium myrtillus*

**Characteristics:** a small shrub, up to 50 cm in height with erect green, angular shoots. The leaves are ovate to ovate-elliptical, with finely toothed margins, the underside slightly hairy. The almost spherical or pitcher-shaped flowers appear singly in the leaf axils in May-June; they are pale greenish-white with a reddish tinge. The fruits (below) are blue-black, with a whitish-blue bloom, with a pleasant taste and coloured juice.—**Distribution:** Europe and western Asia. Common in Britain. Also known as Blaeberry, Whortleberry.

## Bog Whortleberry *Vaccinium uliginosum*

**Characteristics:** a small shrub with erect, cylindrical shoots. The shoots are ovate to elliptical with untoothed margins, the underside with a prominent network of veins. The whitish-pink, pitcher-shaped flowers appear in May-June (above, right). The fruits are blue-black, sweetish but insipid, with colourless juice.—**Distribution:** Europe, western Asia, North America. A common plant in northern England and the Scottish Highlands.

# Ling *Calluna vulgaris*

**Characteristics:** an evergreen shrub up to 20-50 cm in height, rarely to 100 cm. The shoots are procumbent to erect. The leaves are longish-ovate, 2-3 mm long, overlapping like roof tiles. The pink, rarely white, flowers appear in July-October on long, erect shoots (above and below, left).—**Distribution:** Europe and western Asia, on acid soils. A very abundant plant in Britain. Also known as Heather.

# Cross-leaved Heath *Erica tetralix*

**Characteristics:** a small, evergreen, erect shrub up to 50 cm in height. The shoots are pale brown and hairy. The leaves, which are arranged in fours, are needle-shaped, 3-5 mm long, the margins with short stiff hairs. The pink, more rarely white, nodding flowers appear in June-September in small terminal clusters of 5-12 (below, right).—**Distribution:** Europe. An abundant plant in many parts of Britain, particularly in the west, on damp moorland, and always on calcium-free soils.

The Mediterranean Heath (*Erica carnea*) is an evergreen shrub up to 30 cm in height which has flesh-coloured to carmine flowers in February-April and sometimes October-December. The flowers have dark brown stamens which protrude from the corolla. Europe, in scattered localities, such as the Alps and also in boggy areas in Mayo and Galway in Ireland. The life span is 30 years or more.

# Common Ash  *Fraxinus excelsior*

**Characteristics:** a tree up to 40 m in height, which may live for about 300 years and would then have a trunk circumference of 3 m or more. The crown is roundish, and there are often no branches on the lower part of the trunk. The bark is at first grey to yellowish-grey and very smooth, later becoming darker and ridged. The twigs are pale grey. The leaves are opposite and pinnate, up to 30 cm long, with 7-12 (usually 11) longish-lanceolate, pointed, toothed leaflets, each 7-11 cm long (above), their undersides with white down on each side of the central nerve. The buds (fig. 3) are black to blackish-brown. The flowers appear in April-May, before the leaves, in dense clusters (below, left). The fruits are flat and winged, 3-4 cm long (below, right), and they remain on the tree over winter; they are known as keys.—**Distribution:** Europe and western Asia. A native tree in Britain, where it is common, particularly on damp soils in places where the light is good. Frequently planted in city parks. The timber is very elastic and is used for making skis.

The Manna Ash (*F. ornus*) is usually a smaller tree, 4-8 m in height, with a much branched crown and smooth, brownish to greenish bark. The leaves are up to 20 cm long, usually with 7 stalked longish-ovate leaflets. The creamy-white, fragrant flowers appear in May. This tree, also known as Flowering Ash, is native to southern Europe and Anatolia, and was introduced into Britain before 1700.

# Privet  *Ligustrum vulgare*

**Characteristics:** a dense shrub up to about 15 m in height, with opposite, longish-lanceolate to longish-ovate, smooth leaves, 3-6 × 1-2 cm; sometimes evergreen. The buds are ovate, green to red-brown (fig. 106), with fine hairs. The whitish, sweetly scented flowers (above) appear in June-July in short, compact clusters. The fruit is a blackberry, about the size of a pea (below, left), and poisonous.—**Distribution:** Europe and western Asia. Common in southern England, mainly in chalk districts. The species *L. ovalifolium* is commonly used for hedging.

The juice from the fruits was at one time used for colouring leather and the timber is very suitable for turnery.

# Bittersweet  *Solanum dulcamara*

**Characteristics:** a climbing or straggling sub-shrub up to 3 m in height (the uppermost shoots die off in winter), with hollow, greyish-yellow branches. The leaves are ovate to heart-shaped and pointed, smooth and entire. The upper leaves often have three lobes and the central lobe is then always much larger than the laterals (fig. 20). The flowers, which are violet with yellow anthers, appear in June-July in clusters (below, right). The fruits are small, spherical berries which are red and poisonous. The taste is at first bitter, then sweet.—**Distribution:** Europe. Widely distributed in England and Ireland, less so in Scotland.

# Elders  *Sambucus*

**Characteristics:** shrubs, more rarely small trees with pith-filled branches and opposite, pinnate leaves. The leaflets are regularly toothed. The numerous small white flowers are in broad, flat clusters. Each berry-like fruit contains eight or fewer seed-like stones, each with a single seed.


# Common Elder  *Sambucus nigra*

**Characteristics:** a shrub (above, right) or small tree up to 6 (-12) m in height. The pith of the young shoots is white, the branches grey to pale grey-brown, densely beset with large cork cells. The bark is deeply furrowed and corky. The pinnate leaves have 3-7, usually 5 ovate-elliptical to ovate-lanceolate, pointed leaflets, each 10-15 cm long. The buds (fig. 107) are green to reddish. The yellowish-white, heavily scented flowers appear in June-August in clusters 10-20 cm across (above, left). The fruits are shiny black when ripe (below, left).—**Distribution:** Europe. Widespread in England and Ireland where it is probably native, but apparently only introduced into Scotland. The fruits are edible in the form of a jelly made with other fruits, such as blackberries.


# Red-berried Elder  *Sambucus racemosa*

**Characteristics:** a shrub up to 2-3 m in height. The pith of the young shoots is yellow-brown. The leaves are similar to those of the preceding species, but the leaflets are usually only 4-6 cm long. The buds are spherical to ovate, the scales green with brown edges, often with a violet tinge, the terminal buds often in pairs (fig. 108). The greenish-yellow to yellowish flowers appear in April-May. The fruits are bright red (below, right), about 5 mm in diameter.—**Distribution:** Europe and eastwards to China. Not native to Britain, where it is, however, planted as an ornamental shrub.

# Guelder Rose  *Viburnum opulus*

**Characteristics:** a shrub up to 4 m in height. The bark is thin, pale grey, becoming scaly with age, and the shoots are smooth. The leaves are opposite, with 3-5 lobes, up to about 12 × 10 cm, coarsely toothed, the underside downy. The slender petioles are 1-2 cm long with large glands at the top (fig. 30). The leaves turn wine-red in autumn. The lateral buds are longish-ovate, pointed, smooth with two scales and short stalks (fig. 109). The white flowers (above, left) appear in May-June in broad clusters. The marginal flowers lack stamens and styles and are therefore sterile, but they serve to attract insects which may pollinate the central fertile flowers. The fruits are shiny red (above, right), about 1 cm long.—**Distribution:** Europe and western Asia, up to altitudes of 1,400 m. A common shrub in England and Ireland, less so in Scotland. The fruits are not edible.

# Wayfaring Tree  *Viburnum lantana*

**Characteristics:** a shrub up to about 5 m in height. The young shoots are densely covered with a soft, mealy down. The leaves are opposite, ovate, finely toothed, dark green above, downy below. The buds are white to greyish and downy, with the leaf and flower rudiments already recognizable (fig. 4). The white flowers appear in broad clusters in May-June (below, left) and the fruits are ovate, at first red then deep black (below, right) and about 8 mm long.—**Distribution:** Europe and Asia Minor, along the edges of woods and on rocky slopes, particularly in chalk districts. A fairly common plant on suitable soils in England as far north as Yorkshire, but probably not native further north or in Scotland.

# Perfoliate Honeysuckle
## Lonicera caprifolium

**Characteristics:** a scrambling or climbing shrub up to 10 m in height, with opposite, elliptical to ovate leaves, 4-10 cm long, the underside pale bluish-green. The uppermost pairs of leaves are fused at the base to form an almost circular disc (above, and fig. 22). The buds are longish, pointed, distinctly keeled and often unequal in size (fig. 110). The yellowish-white flowers, with a reddish tinge, appear in May-June within a pair of fused leaves (above). Each individual flower is 3-4 cm long and strongly scented, particularly in the early evening. The fruits are bright red.—**Distribution:** central and south-eastern Europe. Not a native plant in Britain, but widely planted and more or less naturalized in England and some parts of Scotland.

The very similar Common Honeysuckle or Woodbine (*L. periclymenum*) is a woody, climbing shrub up to 3-4 m in height, but the uppermost leaf pairs are never fused. The flowers, which are similar to those of the preceding species, appear in July-August. The shoots are smooth, but with glands near the buds (fig. 111).—**Distribution:** Europe. Abundant throughout Britain.

# Fly Honeysuckle   *Lonicera xylosteum*

**Characteristics:** an erect shrub up to 3 m in height, with downy shoots. The leaves are opposite, roundish-elliptical (fig. 21), 3-6 cm long, and particularly downy on the underside. The buds are longish, pointed, downy and yellowish-brown to grey-brown (fig. 112). The scentless flowers, which are at first white, later yellow and about 1 cm long, appear in May-June, always two together on a common hairy stalk (below, left). The fruits are bright scarlet, always two close together (below, right).—**Distribution:** Europe and western Asia. A widely distributed plant, usually as an escape from gardens, but it may be native in one area of Sussex.

# Index

## English Names

6616

# Latin Names